Presented to

From

Date

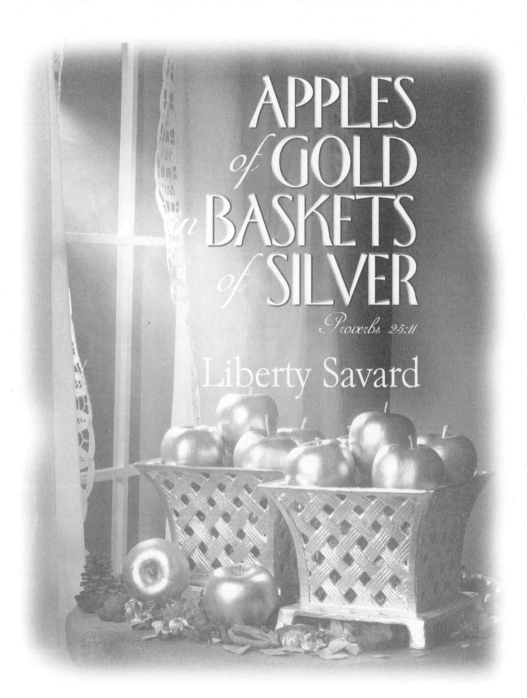

APPLES
of GOLD
in BASKETS
of SILVER

Proverbs 25:11

Liberty Savard

Bridge-Logos

Gainesville, Florida 32614 USA

APPLES OF GOLD IN BASKETS OF SILVER
by Liberty Savard

International Standard Book Number: 0-88270-9070-9089
Library of Congress Catalog Card Number: Pending

Bridge-Logos

Gainesville, FL 32614
bridgelogos.com

DEDICATION

I would like to dedicate this first *Apples of Gold In Baskets of Silver* to my publisher, Guy Morrell, to my designer, Andy Toman, and to my typesetter, Suzi Toman. These friends have all made the process of publishing this book special for me.

INTRODUCTION

Being a writer does not mean that you just write books. A writer is also an information pack rat—perpetually accumulating interesting facts, provocative thoughts, good phrases, and unusual statistics. At times my office and my house both look as if paper tigers live and reproduce there. I cut out paragraphs from articles, clip out one liners from stories, jot down comments I hear on the television, and make notes from headlines in the newspaper which all accumulate in a very ordinary brown box until I am ready to start a new manuscript. Then I begin to pull the scraps of paper and notes out of the box for inspiration.

Although careful construction is involved in writing a book, writing is not like building a house or assembling a car engine. A good contractor and a top mechanic know exactly what they expect to end up with when they have completed the assembling of their different materials. As a writer, I rarely know exactly what I will end up with. I respond to and undergo change in my own life related to what I am writing. As I practice what I'm writing, the book and I both continue to be a work in progress.

There has never been one book that allowed me to use so many of the tidbits in my brown box of inspiration as this one. Writing *Apples of Gold in Baskets of Silver* has been like a glorious treasure hunt for me. Writing a collection of daily teachings is very different than writing within the continuity of a regular book. Writing this book has been time consuming, but it has also been very stimulating. It has also been very difficult for me to capture and contain a daily that I did not want to write any others. Writing a magazine article seems like trying to float a cruise ship of ideas down a tiny canal to this writes who tends to write like the floating of a navy down the Nile River!

As I have written this book, I have undergone a fierce soul inventory during the process. Researching five different versions of the Bible as well as many commentaries, Bible dictionaries, and word studies, I have been personally challenged by every Golden Apple and every Tasting The Truth question I have written. I could not write these pages without examining myself to see if I was working on every area that I was challenging the reader with. If not, that area of challenge became my focus for days.

Proverbs 25:11 is a lovely verse in every Bible translation I have ever read, but I have chosen to use *The Living Bible* version for the title of this collection of 100 daily teachings, questions, and prayer from the Word: *"Timely advice is as lovely as gold apples in a silver basket"* (Provers 25:11, *TLB*). It is my hope that you will read this collection for encouragement, new understanding, revealing of misunderstandings, and revealing of hidden things your soul has denied.

This collection is designed for both personal and group study. The book is broken down into ten Baskets with each Basket containing ten progressive teachings, or Golden Apples, on one subject. You or a group can focus on all ten of the teachings to get an indepth feel of the subject in that Basket. Or, if you or a group wants variety in teaching, then choose to study a Golden Apple from each of the ten Baskets. There are no days, weeks, or months to adhere to. This book can be picked up and read on any page for inspiration for a certain situation, or it can be read in order each day.

Just enjoy the fruit within these covers. Chew it well and let it nourish your soul. God bless you as you begin your time with *Apples of Gold in Baskets of Silver.*

CONTENTS

1

Silver Basket

PRAISE HIM

Golden Apple One

Praise Him For Your Spiritual Blood Transfusion

"I praise you because I am fearfully and wonderfully made; your works are wonderful, I know that full well. My frame was not hidden from you when I was made in the secret place. When I was woven together in the depths of the earth, your eyes saw my unformed body. All the days ordained for me were written in your book before one of them came to be."

(Psalm 139:14-16, *NIV*)

Each one of us was born into a different set of family dynamics and circumstances. Some were born to parents who did not know how to love or nurture. Some were born into discouraged families, some into performance-oriented families, and some into wildly dysfunctional families. When you are living in the world without Jesus, these generational liabilities can shred your soul, eating away at your sense of worth and identity.

Non-believers often spend their entire lives trying to overcome this generational lack. The Good News is that when you became a Christian, you were born into a new family with a new spiritual parent and bloodline! You can discard the effects and influences of all of your unmet needs, unhealed hurts, and unresolved questions and receive God's perfected plans for your life. No longer do you have to live under any generational liabilities.

God sent His Son, Jesus Christ, to give you everything you need to become a new creature—love, joy, hope, wholeness, and purpose. You can receive them today.

Father God, thank you for watching over me when I did not know or care who you were. I bind my will to your will, Lord, and my mind to the mind of Christ. I loose all of the former patterns of thinking and wrong beliefs I have ever had. I am ready to live with a new bloodline and new attitudes towards life and others. Thank you. In Jesus' Name, Amen.

Tasting The Truth

What can happen to non-believers who came from families with generational liabilities?

_____

_____

What is different between the non-believers above and the Christian believers who came out of the same kinds of family dynamics?

_____

_____

Do you need to forgive someone in your family? If so, write a short note to God here about why you haven't done that yet.

_____

_____

_____

What effects and influences of past hurts still bother you today? Are you willing to ask God for grace and mercy and healing so you can give them to Him? If so, stop and ask Him right now. Then write down what He says.

_____

_____

_____

I bind my will to your will, Father. I bind my mind to your mind, Jesus. I bind myself to the truth of your Word and all it tells me about how much you love me. I thank you and praise you, Father, for who you are and what you have done. You are my Father in heaven who lives within my born-again spirit. Help me recognize where I have not yet let Jesus Christ's blood transfusion enter, all of the places where I still feel scorched and raw. I want to be whole and ready to tell others why I praise you, why I love you, and why I need you so much. Blessings and honor to you, Lord. Amen.

APPLES of GOLD
in BASKETS
of SILVER
Proverbs 25:11

Golden Apple Two

Praise Him For Today

"Shout for joy to the LORD, all the earth. Worship the LORD with gladness; come before him with joyful songs. Know that the LORD is God. It is he who made us, and we are his; we are his people, the sheep of his pasture. Enter his gates with thanksgiving and his courts with praise; give thanks to him and praise his name. For the LORD is good and his love endures forever; his faithfulness continues through all generations."

(Psalm 100, *NIV*)

When my days are not as bright as they could be and my heart is not rejoicing as it should be, I remind myself of an old song I learned in the early 1970's: *"This is the day that the Lord has made. I will rejoice and be glad in it."* Right after that song, I learned to sing, *"I will enter His gates with thanksgiving in my heart, I will enter His courts with praise."* These words remind me that every new day is a gift from God. I will rejoice in each one with thanksgiving and praise. This is a choice that I must make each day.

When my days are so difficult that they bleed over into my nights, then I will choose (at 2:00 a.m. or whenever I'm awakened by feelings of anxiety or pending disaster) to tell myself that my God is in control. Because I have chosen to bind myself to His will, I have committed my life to His control as well. I'm always grateful for the binding and loosing prayers when these ragged moments tear into my sleep or prevent it. I am reminded that I'm the apple of His eye.

Lord, you are worthy, you are mighty, you are holy. You alone are great and filled with glory. How incredible and amazing that you have chosen to share yourself with me, day and night. I am speechless at the glory of your generosity and love. I am unable to express my love and gratitude back to you, so I just say thank you. Amen.

Tasting The Truth

What can you thank Him for and praise Him for today?

_____

_____

_____

Each new day that God gives you is a what?

_____

_____

What have you been doing about overcoming anxiety? Do you feel it has been productive?

_____

_____

_____

The next time you wake up at night feeling anxious, pray and bind your mind to the mind of Christ and loose all wrong patterns of thinking. Remind yourself that He is in control. Do this as often as you have to until you fall asleep. Then write in here how you felt.

_____

_____

Lord, you deserve all glory and honor. I lift my heart up to you in worship and adoration. There is no one else like you. This is the day that you have made—all 24 hours of it. I bind myself—mind, will, and emotions— to your will and your plans. I cannot always seem to fend off the thoughts that come when I am under pressure or it is dark and cold outside, but I can reaffirm my trust and confidence that you are with me every minute. I can trust every detail of my life to you. How incredible that you have chosen to choose me and honor me with your love. Thank you for your faithfulness towards me, my Lord. Amen.

APPLES of GOLD
in BASKETS
of SILVER
Proverbs 25:11

Golden Apple Three

Praise Him In The Morning

"Rejoice in the Lord always. Again I will say, rejoice . . . Be anxious for nothing, but in everything by prayer and supplication, with thanksgiving, let your requests be made known to God; and the peace of God, which surpasses all understanding, will guard your hearts and minds through Christ Jesus."

(Philippians 4:4-7, *NKJV*)

Thank the Lord God Almighty for this morning. Thank Him for His majesty and creative power. He is in control and He is good. He loves you and is watching over you. Declare that this day is going to be a **worry-free zone**! Hallelujah! *"Today is the day the Lord hath made; let us rejoice and be glad in it"* (Psalms 118:24, *KJV*).

Lift up your praises to Him, wrapping yourself in His promises of love. If God is for you, who can be against you? Regardless of the troubles you went to bed with last night, God is still in charge of your life if you let Him be. He is entirely capable of making this day worry free for you. He reigns in the big things and He reigns in the smallest details of your life. He is your strength and salvation in the good times and in the dark times.

His peace will settle in your soul if you make room for it. Peace is a gentle gift that will not fight the fears of your soul for position within you. Prepare a place within yourself to receive it. Be still before Him and pray Revelation 5:12-13:

You are worthy, Jesus, you are the Lamb who was slain for the sins of the world. My Savior, you are worthy to receive power and wealth and wisdom and strength and honor and glory and praise! To Almighty God who sits on the throne and to the Lamb ever beside Him be praise and honor and glory and power, for ever and ever! Amen.

Tasting The Truth

What do I need to loose from my soul to make today a worry-free zone?

_____

_____

_____

What can I rejoice about right now, this very day?

_____

_____

_____

_____

What has the noonday sun revealed in my soul?

_____

_____

_____

Do you really believe He reigns in all things? If you do, then why do you think your life can seem to slide sideways at times?

_____

_____

_____

What can you say right now to honor Jesus?

_____

_____

_____

I will rejoice in you always, Lord. I will rejoice in your mighty works and your creation. I will rejoice in your faithfulness. I will rejoice in this day. I have nothing to be anxious about because you are with me. I will therefore thank you for what you know I need, I do not need to tell you. I am grateful that you are in control of the world without and of my soul within to the degree that I have surrendered it to you. I am grateful for your peace that you have sent to guard my heart and mind. I am grateful for the air I can breathe and for the strength you have given to me. Praise your name, Amen.

APPLES of GOLD
in BASKETS
of SILVER
Proverbs 25:11

Golden Apple Four

Praise Him At Noon Time

"But as for me, I will always have hope; I will praise you more and more. My mouth will tell of your righteousness, of your salvation all day long, though I know not its measure. I will come and proclaim your mighty acts, O Sovereign LORD; I will proclaim your righteousness, yours alone."

(Psalm 71:14-16, *NIV*)

Stand up at noontime with the sun over your head, and raise your smiling face and outstretched arms to Him. Lift up your voice to Him with words of honor and love and adoration. He has made you for himself, you are the workmanship of His hands—created to love and adore Him. Tell Him that you love Him with all the love you know how to give.

"Whatever things are true, whatever things are noble, whatever things are just, whatever things are pure, whatever things are lovely, whatever things are of good report, if there is any virtue and if there is anything praiseworthy— meditate on these things" (Philippians 4:8, *NKJV*). Meditating on His goodness and power and love in the middle of the day is a good way to focus your mind on things above.

"Commit your way to the LORD; trust in him and he will do this: He will make your righteousness shine like the dawn, the justice of your cause like the noonday sun" (Psalm 37:5-6, *NIV*). The sun shines brightest right above us when it is noon. There is no darkness to be seen, no hidden things or shadows in the light of the noonday sun. Thank Him for the light to walk in as you follow the paths He's planned beforehand for you.

Praise you, gracious Lord, all thanksgiving and honor to you who has set the sun in the sky and the Son in my heart. Thank you for your wondrous plans and your mighty purposes. Thank you for allowing me to be in your family. Amen.

Tasting The Truth

What can you tell the Lord that you love about Him today?

_____

_____

_____

What things of good report can you meditate on today?

_____

_____

_____

_____

Is there something you can commit to Him today and believe that He will change the outcome for better?

_____

_____

_____

_____

_____

What has He shined His light on in your life that used to be dark and frightening?

_____

_____

_____

APPLES of GOLD in BASKETS of SILVER Proverbs 25:11

You are my Shepherd and my Savior, and you lead me in paths of light. Thank you for lighting my way in a world that has so much darkness. Today I will focus on thinking on things that are noble, just, pure, lovely, and of good report. I will meditate on your virtue and I will praise you for being an example to me so I can run the race to become more like you. I need you to make my righteousness shine like the noonday sun today. I need your light so I can see that you have truly chosen me. Amen.

Golden Apple Five

Praise Him In The Evening

"From the rising of the sun to the place where it sets, the name of the LORD is to be praised. The LORD is exalted over all the nations, his glory above the heavens. Who is like the LORD our God, the One who sits enthroned on high, who stoops down to look on the heavens and the earth? He raises the poor from the dust and lifts the needy from the ash heap; he seats them with princes, with the princes of their people."

(Psalm 113:3-8, *NIV*)

The evening is a time of twilight and dusky shadows, not day but not fully night. It is a time to consider one's life that lies ahead and the day that has just finished. God came and walked in the cool of the evening in the Garden of Eden looking for Adam. Evening is a good time to meet with God. Let the day slow down and walk and talk with your God.

It is good to stop and meditate on the ways of God, to ask Him to search your heart. "*Every day I review the ways he works; I try not to miss a trick. I feel put back together, and I'm watching my step. God rewrote the text of my life when I opened the book of my heart to his eyes*" (Psalm 18:22-24, *The Message*).

In the evening, thank the Lord that another day is drawing to a close but you have this time to spend with Him. Rest in Him and do not fret that you did not get everything done. Perhaps you got done what He wanted, and now He wants a part of your day just for himself. Give it to Him and be honored He cares enough to want that time with you. The Word says that you are the apple of His eye and He guards you (Deuteronomy 32:10). He keeps you safe through the day and the night.

As I contemplate the end of this day, I will choose to spend time with you. What do you want to speak to me about today? I want to learn to listen, Father. I want to hear your voice. Amen.

Tasting The Truth

Are you amazed that the Lord would stoop down to look on the earth and find you? Why?

_____

_____

_____

As your day begins to end, can you imagine God coming down to meet with you? What would you say to Him if He walked up to you right now?

_____

_____

_____

_____

Review some of the works and ways of God that you know.

_____

_____

_____

Can you believe that God doesn't really care about what you didn't get done today, that He only wants part of what's left? Explain your answer

_____

_____

_____

_____

APPLES of GOLD
in BASKETS
of SILVER
Proverbs 25:11

Precious Lord, I want to give you the rest of my day. I am amazed that you would care. You must be very, very busy running the whole earth. What have you wanted to tell me today? Will you teach me how to hear your voice? Will you teach me how to shut out the clamor and clanging of the world around me? Dear Father, I am so grateful for your love. Amen.

Golden Apple Six

Praise Him For His Plans For You

"We thank you, God, we thank you—your Name is our favorite word; your mighty works are all we talk about. You say, 'I'm calling this meeting to order, I'm ready to set things right. When the earth goes topsy-turvy and nobody knows which end is up, I nail it all down, I put everything in place again.'"

(Psalm 75:1-3, *The Message*)

How wonderful to know that God is in charge of everything, that He is the Master builder of all. How grateful you can be that His long arm is never too short to reach you wherever you are. *"He's the One from east to west; from desert to mountains, he's the One. God rules: he brings this one down to his knees, pulls that one up on her feet"* (Psalm 75:6-7, *The Message*).

He watches your every move even when you insist upon going away from Him. He may let you walk away from His paths to teach you important things, but He goes with you.

Everything around us holds together and works together in a finely balanced manner. Every person in the body of Christ is necessary and has a good work to accomplish in God's grand scheme of things. Yet He is a God of both unity and community. He has us work in families, in churches, and in friendships that we would bless both Him and others.

Praise Him that none of us have been called to walk out our destinies in isolation. Praise Him that there are no members of His family who are not important to His big picture. Still, God is far more interested in your relationship with Him than He is in what you are destined to do for His Kingdom.

I am blessed to be part of your big picture, and to yet know that you care about my very small contribution. Thank you for loving me, for watching over me, and for adopting me. Amen.

Tasting The Truth

Is there something you want God to nail down and put in its place?

_____

_____

_____

_____

_____

Can you sense that His arm is always near you? How?

_____

_____

_____

What good work do you think you have been created to accomplish in God's grand Master Plan?

_____

_____

_____

_____

Are you unhappy with your relationship with God? What would make you happier?

_____

_____

_____

_____

APPLES of GOLD
in BASKETS
of SILVER
Proverbs 25:11

Lord, you are in charge of everything, I know that. But sometimes I feel like I'm forgotten at the bottom of your toolbox. Why do I feel that way every now and then? Do I not believe your Word? Help me to understand. I want to be a part of your community plan. I want to work with others, make plans with others. Show me where I fit in and how I am a part. I love being able to talk to you. Thank you for your love. Amen.

Golden Apple Seven

Praise And Bless Him, O My Soul

*"Praise the LORD, O my soul; all my inmost being, praise his holy name.
Praise the LORD, O my soul, and forget not all his benefits—who forgives all
your sins and heals all your diseases, who redeems your life from the pit and
crowns you with love and compassion, who satisfies your desires with good
things so that your youth is renewed like the eagle's."*

(Psalm 103:1-5, *NIV*)

Nearly every use of the word "heart" in the Old Testament comes
from the two Hebrew words *leb* and *lebab,* generally meaning the
intellect, the feelings, and the will—the soul. The word heart as
used in the New Testament comes from the Greek word *kardia* which usually
means the thoughts and the feelings—the soul. It is with our soul that we are
to bless and praise our God.

Matthew Henry said: "We make nothing of our religious performances if we do
not make <u>heart-work</u> of them, if that which is within us, nay, if all that is within
us, be not engaged in them. The work requires the inward man, the whole
man" O Lord, I know I must make heart-work worship rise up to you.

Soul, you will bless Him with all that is within you. You will bless Him with
your mind and all of its thoughts, with your feelings and all of your emotions,
with your will and all of its choices. I will love Him and honor Him and bless
Him with every fiber of my being. I will give thanks for all of His many benefits
to me, reinforcing His benefits to you, my soul, so that you will not forget them.
I will remind you, my soul, over and over of them all.

*Many are your blessings and kindnesses towards me, Father God. How grateful
I am, how blessed I am. You are my life and my reason for living. Bless your
holy name. Amen.*

Tasting The Truth

Make a list of His benefits that your soul must never forget.

_____

_____

_____

What does the word "heart" generally mean in the Old and New Testaments.

_____

_____

_____

What does the phrase "heart-work" mean to you?

_____

_____

Why do you think you need to reinforce His benefits to your soul?

_____

_____

What are you going to remind your soul of, over and over?

_____

_____

What part of us do we need to train to bless God?

_____

_____

APPLES of GOLD
in BASKETS
of SILVER
Proverbs 25:11

You have forgiven my sins and you are healing my diseases and I am grateful. Bless your name, Lord God. You have redeemed me from the pit. I cannot even imagine what that really means, but thank you that I will not have to know. I will make my soul learn to bless you and praise you and rehearse all of the benefits you have given to me. I love you very, very much. I want to honor you with all of my life. Amen.

Golden Apple Eight

Praise Him For His Son

"How blessed is God! And what a blessing he is! He's the Father of our Master, Jesus Christ, and takes us to the high places of blessing in him. Long before he laid down earth's foundations, he had us in mind, had settled on us as the focus of his love, to be made whole and holy by his love."

(Ephesians 1:3-6, *The Message*)

*I*n the synagogue in Nazareth, Jesus read from the scroll of Isaiah: *"The Spirit of the Lord is on me, because he has anointed me to preach good news to the poor. He has sent me to proclaim freedom for the prisoners and recovery of sight for the blind, to release the oppressed, to proclaim the year of the Lord's favor"* (Luke 4:18-19, *NIV*).

Praise God for the gift of freedom and forgiveness in His Son. Jesus Christ has released the oppressed from the heavy yoke of the Law. He also releases us from the religious traditions of man. His Word is filled with truth that shows us how to sift the traditions of man out of the spiritual teachings of today. *"To the Jews who had believed him, Jesus said, 'If you hold to my teaching, you are really my disciples. Then you will know the truth, and the truth will set you free'"* (John 8:31-21, *NIV*).

"whoever lives by the truth comes into the light, so that it may be seen plainly that what he has done has been done through God" (John 3:21, *NIV*). When you know the truth, you cannot be fooled with the fake, and the counterfeit traditions and religion of man will never satisfy you. When you choose to live by the truth, you walk in light for all to see.

Lord, I praise you and thank you for making sure I would have your guidance and instruction every time I pick up your Word. I want to be a good student of your Word. Praises to you, blessing to you, and all my gratitude is yours. Amen.

16

Tasting The Truth

Tell Him how it makes you feel that His Word says that long before He made the earth, He had you in mind.

_____

_____

_____

Can you see yourself as a prisoner who once was blind and oppressed? If not, how do you see yourself as you used to be?

_____

_____

What traditions of man do you feel you should pray about?

_____

_____

_____

Is there anything fake or counterfeit in your life that you don't know what to replace it with? Pray and ask Him to show you. Write down what He says.

_____

_____

Briefly describe here, as if you were talking to a non-believer, what it means to live by the truth and be in the light.

_____

_____

APPLES of GOLD
in BASKETS
of SILVER
Proverbs 25:11

Lord, show me if I have any counterfeits in my life. I know that if I am deceived, there is a very real chance that the deception is hidden from me. I want to walk in your truth and the light that comes from that. I'm ready for a soulish spring housecleaning, Lord. Thank you for the freedom and the forgiveness you have given to me. Thank you, Jesus, for lifting the heavy burdens off me. Your yoke truly is easy and light. I want to know more about you, Lord. Teach me. Amen.

Golden Apple Nine

Praise Him For Your New Self

"I beseech you therefore, brethren, by the mercies of God, that you present your bodies a living sacrifice, holy, acceptable to God, which is your reasonable service. And do not be conformed to this world, but be transformed by the renewing of your mind, that you may prove what is that good and acceptable and perfect will of God."

(Romans 12:1-2, *NKJV*)

*P*raise the Lord that you are being transformed into a new creation. The word transformed comes from the original Greek word *metamorphoo*. This is the same word used to describe the process that turns a caterpillar into a butterfly.

Transformation takes place on the inside, it's never just a sprucing up of the outside. You can shampoo a pig, perfume it, put a silk jacket on it and it might look different. But as soon as it sees mud, it will get back into it. It still has a pig's nature.

God has chosen us to be transformed, to be changed from within so we would no longer be tempted by the mud of our former states. Even when those who are His sin and flop into the mud, He desires to wash them off, shine them up, and tell them that their best days are still ahead of them.

Noah and his family were a fresh start of the process of transformed men and women. Abraham was another fresh start in this process. Then Jacob was another fresh start. But in the New Testament, we have the only sinless fresh start to model our transformation after—Jesus Christ.

Jesus, I want to be transformed. I cannot do it alone, so I bind my will to the will of the Father and I bind myself to the truth of His Word. I loose all desire to go back to my former way of doing anything! I want to go forward with you. Amen.

Tasting The Truth

Are there any areas where you want to be less conformed to the world? Ask Him to show you a better way, and then record what He says.

_____

_____

_____

Where do you think you are in the whole caterpillar/butterfly process?

_____

_____

_____

Are you the same on the inside as you show on the outside? If not, why do you think you are not?

_____

_____

Thank Him here for His faithfulness to us even when we get back in the mud.

_____

_____

Are you aware that you are being watched by many witnesses as being a fresh start? How do you think you are doing?

_____

_____

APPLES of GOLD in BASKETS of SILVER Proverbs 25:11

I am not sure I am ready to be a role model yet, Lord. I want to be, but I still think about the mud sometimes. What makes me do that? I am so grateful for the totally new chance you have given me to become a new creature. I bind myself to you, Lord, putting myself under obligation to your plans and purposes. I loose all old influences and effects of my past out of my soul. I will never turn back and I want to be free from any residue. Thank you, Jesus, for being my hero and my role model. Amen.

Golden Apple Ten

Tell Others To Praise Him For Who He Is

"I've preached you to the whole congregation, I've kept back nothing, God—you know that. I didn't keep the news of your ways a secret, didn't keep it to myself. I told it all, how dependable you are, how thorough. I didn't hold back pieces of love and truth for myself alone. I told it all."

(Psalm 40:9-10, The Message)

*I*f God was to give you every blessing and gift you could possibly ask for, He would still have enough blessings and gifts left to give fifty times as much to you again and to everyone else in the world, too. Then He would only be getting started in handing out His gifts.

The world is full of people who do not feel loved and cherished. The world is full of people who have no apparent blessings, no precious gifts, and no hope that their lives might ever get better. Praise His holy Name that He has chosen you to be a messenger and an ambassador of His Good News to every hopeless, dejected and rejected person you meet. *"We are therefore Christ's ambassadors, as though God were making his appeal through us. We implore you on Christ's behalf: Be reconciled to God"* (2 Corinthians 5:20, *NIV*).

Don't ever hold back and hide what you have been given. A tightly clenched hand is incapable of receiving any more. You must give away what He's given to you to receive more. What will you say in heaven when He asks you, *"What did you do with the grace that I gave to you? Did you invest it into other lives? Where is the return on my investment in you?"*

I will be your Ambassador of Good News. I bind my life to you, and I loose shyness, fear of rejection, pride, and laziness from myself. Show me who and where and I will go because that is what an Ambassador with Good News does. Amen.

Tasting The Truth

How do you feel when you share about the Lord, telling people how dependable He is?

_____

_____

_____

Have you ever wondered if you gave away all of your blessings, would He give you more?

_____

_____

_____

What can you loose out of your soul that would cause you to fear rejection when you try to share about Christ?

_____

_____

_____

_____

Does the fact that He has chosen you to be a messenger and an ambassador of His Good News thrill you or concern you?

_____

_____

_____

I want to share your love and encouragement and hope with others. Help me to get over the struggle within me. I must still have unmet needs and unhealed hurts within my soul and I want to open them up to you. Please heal those areas within me that make me too cautious and nervous about what others think. I want to care only about what you think. I want to be excited about being an ambassador for you. Amen.

Silver Basket

2

KNOW HIM
BY HIS WORD

Golden Apple One

Find Hope In His Word

"For whatever things were written before were written for our learning, that we through the patience and comfort of the Scriptures might have hope."

(Romans 15:4, *NKJV*)

Every time you open the Bible, you can know that it holds some spiritual hope, some word of love to strengthen you right now. Your Bible holds keys to deepening your relationship with Christ—an ever-fresh supply of truth to feed upon.

The Word of God is not a collection of sayings to mechanically read each day to say you have had devotions. It is a chance to peek into the very heart of God, an opportunity to know Him better. Reading the Word is like feeding on the hope and truth of eternity, right in the comfort of your own home. That is amazing when you think about it.

What many need is a new fresh mental attitude about the Bible. First of all, stop reading the Word as a duty. Don't say, *"I have read the Word so I'll be okay today,"* as if you were just swallowing medicine that would inoculate you from the world. The Word is not a pill you take so you can be safe.

Don't allow your soul to distract you from the Word. The lawn can wait, the dishes can wait, and the bill paying can wait until later. Truth, hope, equipping for good works, and getting to know Jesus better are waiting for you right now on His Word.

Father, I do need a new attitude about the Bible. I am never going to consider reading your Word as a duty again. I am going to consider it a chance to hear the words you wanted me to hear today. I will be blessed and honored that you always planned I would hear them right on time, even though you formed them before the foundation of the world. Amen.

Tasting The Truth

What can you hope to find in the Bible every time you read it?

_____

_____

What is the Word of God not?

_____

_____

What does the Word give you chance to do?

_____

_____

Reading the Word is like feeding on what?

_____

_____

What do you need if you have been thinking of reading the Word of God as a duty?

_____

_____

What are some of the distractions that you know your soul uses when you are trying to read the Word?

_____

_____

APPLES of GOLD in BASKETS of SILVER Proverbs 25:11

I am going to have a fresh, new mental attitude about reading your Word. I am going to stop considering it my duty, my obligation, and I am going to consider it an opportunity. I want to find new truth and new reason to be encouraged. It is so awesome that I can read your letters to me in my own home. Holy Spirit, teach me to read the Word with fresh eyes so that I would know that the Word is alive and powerful. Amen.

Golden Apple Two

Find Freedom In His Word

*"Anyone who listens to the word but does not do what it says is like a man
who looks at his face in a mirror and, after looking at himself, goes away
and immediately forgets what he looks like. But the man who looks intently
into the perfect law that gives freedom, and continues to do this,
not forgetting what he has heard, but doing it
—he will be blessed in what he does."*

(James 1:23-25, *NIV*)

God says to call on Him and He will rescue, protect, answer, and deliver us from trouble. First we call, then He rescues. He says that as we walk with Him, we will learn to listen to His guidance. Even if we do not seem to hear Him, nor do we feel we can see the path He is showing us, He says, *"I will lead the blind by ways they have not know, along unfamiliar paths I will guide them; I will turn the darkness into light before them and make the rough places smooth"* (Isaiah 42:16, *NIV*).

First Thessalonians 1:5, *The Message*, records Paul telling the Thessalonian Christians, *"When the Message we preached came to you, it wasn't just words. Something happened in you. The Holy Spirit put steel in your convictions."* The King James Version says that the Gospel came to us in power, in the Holy Ghost, and in much assurance. That word assurance in this verse means complete confidence or backbone.

Don't be one who looks into the mirror of the Word and then turns away and forgets what you have seen. Feed your soul with the Word to give it a complete transformation. Wash your soul with the Word to make it sleek and clean. Do this now and be strong and ready for whatever God asks you to do.

It is a blessing, Father, to know that you will guide me on the unfamiliar paths, turning darkness into light before me. I need you so much in every area of my life. Thank you. Amen.

Tasting The Truth

What has God said He would do if we would call on Him?

_____

_____

_____

_____

Even if we do not seem to see the path He is showing us, what has He said He will do?

_____

_____

_____

_____

What does First Thessalonians 1:5 say that the Good News and the Holy Spirit together accomplished in the believers? What does that mean to you?

_____

_____

_____

_____

What does feeding on and washing the Word do for your soul?

_____

_____

_____

_____

I bind my mind to your mind, Jesus. I am going to do this to stabilize my mind so that it cannot play leap frog when I'm trying to read your Word. I want to read your Word, hear your Word, and then do what it says. I want to look intently at the perfect law of the love of Jesus and be set free. Thank you for leading me when I cannot see and the path is unfamiliar. Thank you for your light and for making the rough places smooth. I want steel and backbone in my convictions. I want complete confidence in what I know of your ways and your Word. and your principles. I want to be ready. Amen.

APPLES of GOLD in BASKETS of SILVER
Proverbs 25:11

Golden Apple Three

Find His Promises In His Word

*"Therefore, remember that formerly you who are Gentiles by birth . . .
through the gospel the Gentiles are heirs together with Israel, members
together of one body, and sharers together in the promise in Christ Jesus."*

(Ephesians 2:11, 19-21; 3:6, *NIV*)

When I was a new Christian, I was often confused by people saying, "Well, bless your heart, you can't claim that Scripture! That was for the Jews, Romans, or the king." I struggled to understand what part of the Bible was for me—a mixed-up Gentile of Scottish, Irish, English, German-Dutch, and Cherokee descent. There were no verses for such a lineage.

But I was sure the Bible was written for me, too. I decided to claim and stand upon any verse of the Bible that encouraged me, strengthened me, or caused me to feel the love of God.

First Kings 8:56 (*NIV*) says, *"Not one word has failed of all the good promises he gave through his servant Moses."*

Romans 8:28 (*NIV*) tells us, *"And we know that in all things God works for the good of those who love him, who have been called according to his purpose."*

John 1:12 (*NIV*) says, *"To all who receive him, to those who believed in his name, he gave the right to become children of God."*

John 14:23 (*NIV*) tells us, *"Jesus replied, 'If anyone loves me, he will obey my teaching. My Father will love him, and we will come to him and make our home with him.'"*

Jesus, thank you that the Father's promises are forever. I am called and His child, and you are both with me. Amen.

Tasting The Truth

What does the Word in Ephesians 2 say has now happened to the Gentile believers?

_____

_____

Why can you be assured that you can claim the promises throughout the whole Bible?

_____

_____

_____

List five of God's promises in His Word that encourage you.

_____

_____

_____

_____

What have you had God do for you to work something seemingly negative to your good?

_____

_____

_____

Jesus has said that He and His Father will love you, come to you, and make their home with you. What do you think that means?

_____

_____

APPLES of GOLD in BASKETS of SILVER Proverbs 25:11

I need more of your Word in me for it both comforts me and gives me hope. Thank you for giving us your written Word, all over the world, so that your people could all be learning and understanding you together. Please see that people in other countries have opportunities to get Bibles in their own languages. And please see that those thousands of people who have Bibles will want to read them and know you. Amen.

Golden Apple Four

Find Discernment For Your Soul In His Word

"For the word of God is living and powerful, and sharper than any two-edged sword, piercing even to the division of soul and spirit, and of joints and marrow, and is a discerner of the thoughts and intents of the heart."

(Hebrews 4:12, *NKJV*)

The Word of God discerns the <u>intents</u> of the heart (soul), the word intent coming from the Greek word *ennoia* which means the thoughts, will, and feelings. If you allow the Word to do its supernatural work, it will cut deeply into your soul to reveal the deception and denial in your thinking. Once that process has begun, the Word will also begin to reveal you as God sees you.

What a powerful diagnostic tool we have in the Scriptures. Why do we struggle so to use them regularly and passionately? When you receive a letter in the mail from an old friend, do you have to make yourself read it? Do you struggle with knowing that you should read it? Probably not. You are more likely to be thrilled to hear what that friend has to say.

Why do we not consider God to be our friend, desiring to read His letters to us so much that we cannot be deterred by any distraction? Is it because our souls fear having their subversive thoughts against the Word of God exposed? The enemy is very aware of the Word's power to cut through his lies as well. He and your soul both work to convince you to read the Word "later" when you have more time. Have you noticed that later often never seems to happen? Reject the word "later" from your vocabulary and connect His Word to your word NOW.

I am sorry for being so careless with your correspondence to me, God. You are my friend and you worked with many men to record your thoughts and ways to read today. I choose to read those words now so I can know you better. Amen.

Tasting The Truth

Why do you think that the Word is compared to a sword?

_____

_____

_____

Have you read the Word and had it suddenly reveal something to you that you did not know? What was it?

_____

_____

_____

Compare a letter from your friend to the Word being letters from God.

_____

_____

_____

_____

What has your soul done to get you to wait until "later"?

_____

_____

_____

Look up John 3:21 and write it here.

_____

_____

_____

APPLES of GOLD
in BASKETS
of SILVER
Proverbs 25:11

I've heard what you are saying to me, Lord, and I will search your Word for new understanding. I will turn to the Word when I need encouragement and use the Word to encourage others as well about who you are and what you have done and are doing. If I struggle to find time to read the Word in my busy schedule, show me what I can cut out of my daily routine to make room for your correspondence to me. I am excited that I am going to keep learning more about you and other wonderful things from the Word. I can't wait. Amen.

Golden Apple Five

Find Encouragement In His Word

"He Himself has said, 'I will never leave you nor forsake you.'
So we may boldly say: 'The LORD is my helper;
I will not fear. What can man do to me?'"

(Hebrews 13:5-6, *NKJV*)

O nce God has welcomed you into His family, He plans for you to remain with Him for all eternity. He has no intentions of allowing Satan to kidnap you, nor is He going to allow you to kidnap yourself. He has purchased you, possesses you, preserves you, and is preparing you for the great purposes you are created to fulfill. What a deal!

Your born-again spirit has no problem with soaking in the Word like a desert wanderer at an oasis. But your soul's half-truths and preconceived ideas about your relationship with Jesus Christ cause it to accept only bits and pieces of the Word. Your soul will reject any part of the Word that threatens its status quo in the control tower of your life, just like a computer program will reject whatever does not agree with its protocols.

If your unsurrendered soul continues to upstage your spirit for control of your life, it will keep your mind from being renewed. It will keep your will from surrendering to God's will, and it will keep your emotions fearfully hiding from the Holy Spirit's healing. You can stop your soul's uprisings and cause it to come into alignment with God's will by filling it with more of God's Word. When you do, you will begin to feel as if you have thrown off a great yoke and you will rejoice!

Jesus, you have brought me into a wonderful place—the middle of the family of God. Thank you so much. I want to surrender my soul to all God has for me. I bind my soul to Him, and I loose its control tactics and strongholds. Thank you for the Keys of the Kingdom that allows me to make it give up. Amen.

Tasting The Truth

What did you learn from this Golden Apple?

_____

_____

God is not about to let Satan kidnap you nor let you kidnap yourself. What does this mean to you?

_____

_____

_____

What is the difference between how your soul and your spirit approach the Word of God?

_____

_____

_____

Why is it dangerous for your soul to keep rejecting parts of the Word?

_____

_____

_____

When you stop your soul's uprisings and make it line up with God's will, how will you feel?

_____

_____

Your promises are strong and true and I thank you for them. I really need to understand the truth of you saying that you will never leave me or forsake me. Your Word says you are my helper, too. That certainly does help me not fear. I want to get over my fear of man, my fear of being criticized and embarrassed. I want to think only about what you think about me. Even then, I won't worry, but I will care. Help me teach my soul to want to soak itself in the Word. Help me get my spirit and my soul on the same track. Amen.

APPLES of GOLD
in BASKETS
of SILVER
Proverbs 25:11

Golden Apple Six

Don't Miss The Mark In His Word

*"Therefore, since we are surrounded by such a cloud of witnesses,
let us throw off everything that hinders and
the sin that so easily entangles, and let us run with
perseverance the race marked out for us."*

(Hebrews 12:1, *NIV*)

The Word of God uses different analogies and metaphors to explain concepts and principles. The above verse uses an athletic analogy, using the word sin (from the Greek word *hamartia* meaning <u>failing to hit the mark</u>) to express the idea of allowing distractions to keep you from winning a race.

We can get entangled with so many "good" things while running our version of the Christian race. Entangled means to be thwarted and kept from running the race you are meant to run. Take stock of the distractions in your life. Do you need to lay aside any relationships, activities, or other things that may be good but not God? Not all good things contribute to your successful running.

Think of the first time you fell in love and how much time you wanted to spend just being near that person. Do you feel that way today about just being <u>with</u> God? Don't let your soul confuse you with the deception that doing things for God is the same as spending time with Him. It's always the right time to return to your true first love. It's always time to sort out the good from the God in your life. Do you have a good balance between your soul's pursuit of self-interests and making sure it is getting to know your Savior better?

I want to know you better, Lord. Please forgive me for allowing my soul to entangle itself in unimportant things. I will run my race to know you. I loose all wrong desires and agendas that my soul would use to try to distract me. I love you. Amen.

Tasting The Truth

What might be entangling you as you run your race?

_____

_____

_____

Is perseverance one of your more enduring traits? How could you begin to train your soul to have more perseverance?

_____

_____

What does it mean to fail to hit the mark?

_____

_____

_____

List both the good things and the God things that you are now doing.

_____

_____

_____

_____

Is it time to lay aside some relationships and activities and return to your first love again?

_____

_____

I do not know how I managed to move away from my first love. I want to return to you, Lord, and put you back in the center of my day, my life. Forgive me for getting so many good things going and thinking that I was spending time with you. Forgive me for trying to pray while I'm driving or working so that I don't feel that I'm wasting time. I love you and I am grateful that you know what frail creatures we are. I so want to show you my love and do things properly, but I'm still not there yet. I will remember the height from which I have fallen! I will repent and do the things I did at first. Amen.

APPLES of GOLD
in BASKETS
of SILVER
Proverbs 25:11

Golden Apple Seven

Practicing His Word

"All Scripture is given by inspiration of God, and is profitable for doctrine, for reproof, for correction, for instruction in righteousness, that the man of God may be complete, thoroughly equipped for every good work."

(2 Timothy 3:16-17, *NKJV*)

God's Word often tells us to do the opposite of what we think we should. God knew that there were many things that we could not possibly understand by our own experiences, so He gave everyone on Earth the opportunity to have a Master Operating Manual for the Abundant Life—His written Word. No one has to go without this Operating Manual!

One important rule of survival in the harsh Australian Outback is that you never leave your vehicle if it breaks down. It is much easier to find a vehicle than a fallen body. Many have died in the Outback because of disregarding that rule. Had they trusted the general truth of that rule and stayed put, most would have been found and lived. Such rules only make sense to people who can believe someone wants to rescue them!

The Word of God tells us that if we have trust and confidence in Him, He will come to our rescue. In fact, He has placed His whole reputation upon the truth of whether or not He keeps His Word. If God so wants to be proven trustworthy, why do we keep coming up with reasons to not trust Him? You are not going to always understand what God is telling you to do in His Word, but study what He's said and do it anyway!

Jesus, it doesn't matter whether or not your Word seems to make sense in the heat of the problems of today—I believe you will make it work on my behalf. I have trust and confidence in your goodness towards me. I can't rescue me, but thank you, Lord, for Jesus already has. Amen.

Tasting The Truth

List a Scripture that seems to be illogical to you. Pray and ask God to help you understand it.

_____

_____

_____

Do you see your Bible as an Operating Manual or a Survival Manual?

_____

_____

Do you believe there is someone somewhere who wants to rescue you? How do you feel about that?

_____

_____

If God is placing His whole reputation on being trusted as keeping His Word, why is so hard sometimes to trust Him?

_____

_____

Can you obey Him even if you don't understand what He wants you to do sometimes? Give an example of when you have, and then explain your answer.

_____

_____

Lord, help me to remember that your thoughts are not my thoughts and your ways are not my ways. I obey and then you will position me in safety and with favor. I am finally learning that I cannot understand you and everything else around me through my personal experiences alone. Thank you for sending me and the whole world your Operating Manual. I am grateful because we really need it. Amen.

Golden Apple Eight

Find The Kingdom of Heaven In His Word

"Blessed are the poor in spirit,
for theirs is the kingdom of heaven."

(Matthew 5:3, *NIV*)

When I was young in the Lord, I heard there was a special blessing for not having any money. I heard that those who had money didn't get God's special attention like the poor did. I happened to be working for a church at that time and was poor as a church mouse. I wanted to feel blessed, but I really didn't.

God did teach me much through those lean times, however. When you have an empty wallet and checking account, and no credit cards, you either learn who your Provider—Employer—Father is, or you will be miserable.

Then I learned that this verse is not talking about money. The word spirit as used in this verse means the mind, will, and emotions—the human soul, the heart of man. The word poor as used here means to voluntarily choose a poverty of the soul. Being poor in soul means you choose to give up your own agendas, you choose to bankrupt your own desires and plans.

Psalms 51:17 says God really prefers a *"broken and a contrite heart* (soul)*"* to sacrifices. *The Message* reads, *"Going through the motions doesn't please you, a flawless performance is nothing to you. I learned God-worship when my pride was shattered. Heart-shattered lives ready for love don't for a moment escape God's notice."* Yes, I want to learn this!

I choose to bankrupt my soul, Jesus, for I want the Father's way only. I bind my mind to your mind, and I loose all personal agendas from myself. I desire that the self-focus of my soul would be shattered that I could give your love without personal motives. Amen

Tasting The Truth

What did you learn from this Golden Apple? Can you use it to make a positive change in your life?

_____

_____

_____

What can you learn from lean times?

_____

_____

_____

What is Matthew 5:3 really talking about instead of what we have thought it meant regarding money?

_____

_____

_____

_____

What does being poor in soul really mean?

_____

_____

_____

What does the phrase "heart-shattered" lives mean to you?

_____

_____

APPLES of GOLD
in BASKETS
of SILVER
Proverbs 25:11

I do need to declare poverty in my soul. I do need to bankrupt its plans and agendas. I want to surrender my soul to you. I want it to be in alignment with your will, being under obligation to your plans and purposes. I want to have a broken and contrite heart that pleases you. I know you are not asking me to be without nice things in my life, just without personal desires and motives. I can do that. Thank you, Lord, for allowing me to learn more about you. Amen.

Golden Apple Nine

Hide His Word In Your Heart

*"I have hidden your word in my heart that I might not sin
against you. Praise be to you, O LORD;
teach me your decrees."*

(Psalm 119:11-12, *NIV*)

The born-again spirit has all access to its Creator and the Living Word. It is the unsurrendered soul of the believer that needs the washing and the strengthening of the power hidden within the Scriptures. People fail, backslide, and even perish for a lack of knowledge of the Word. Yet God has seen to it that the Bible is the most publicized book in the entire world. If only each one printed was faithfully read!

Spiritual error springs forth like weeds when there is no understanding or hunger for the Word. So we must hide God's Word in our hearts whether we have proper teachers or not. If we do not, we can be deceived by the ways of the world. Immorality abounds when there are no true moral guidelines.

God's Word gives clear lines of right and wrong to guide when everyone else may be muddling around in situational ethics and personal self-agendas. The unsurrendered human soul generally tries to block the Father's mercy, grace, and wisdom, but feeding on the Word of God diminishes your soul's ability to block out anything of God. His written Word poured into the soul, coupled with a desire for godly understanding, works its way into the soul's hardness to bring healing and trust.

Jesus, I take full responsibility for having the Word in my heart. I am the only one who will keep me from having this be so. When I do not understand what I need to know in your Word, I ask that you give me wisdom to see the truth. I ask that your Holy Spirit would teach me. Your Word is truth and I believe that you will instruct me with it. Amen.

Tasting The Truth

Why does the unsurrendered soul need the written Word more than the born-again spirit?

_____

_____

_____

Whose fault is it whether we have the Word of God in our hearts or not?

_____

_____

How can the Word protect you from spiritual error?

_____

_____

What do you do if you do not have a good Bible teacher at your church?

_____

_____

What is the difference between the Word and situational ethics?

_____

_____

_____

Immorality abounds when there are no what?

_____

_____

Every day I am hiding your Word in my heart. I know that the Word can keep me in truth. Lord, I don't want to be confused or lacking in understanding. I want to be on track with you. I am so glad that you are my God and that you want a personal relationship with me. You want me to know you and you want me to understand you. That is important to me. Thank you again. Amen.

Golden Apple Ten

The Promises In His Word Are Astounding

"I tell you the truth, <u>anyone</u> who has faith in me will do what I have been doing. He will do even greater things than these, because I am going to the Father."

(John 14:12, *NIV*)

What a promise! Man, woman, teenager, child—anyone! Jesus said here that He wants us to be walking on water, stilling storms, raising the dead, opening blind eyes, and more because He has gone back to the Father. There is work unfinished on earth and He's brought us into the Kingdom to finish it.

Jesus left each one of us the Keys of the Kingdom (Matthew 16:19) to use to "put off" every preconceived idea, half-truth, wrong belief, fear, and stronghold within our unsurrendered souls that would keep us from believing that we can do this. Jesus has not asked us to do anything that is not His Father's will.

Ephesians 4:22-24 (*Amplified*), says *"Strip yourselves of your former nature— put off and discard your old unrenewed self . . . Be constantly renewed in the spirit of your mind—having a fresh mental and spiritual attitude; and put on the new nature (the regenerate self) created in God's image."*

Our job is to take these Kingdom keys and use them to get rid of all of our old soul-stuff that needs to be discarded and then bring our bodies, souls, and spirits into alignment with God's perfect will. We need to take off the world's image and put on God's image. We have unfinished Kingdom work to do.

I will have faith that I can do what Jesus said. I bind myself body, soul, and spirit to the Father and I loose all thoughts of pain, failure, and humiliation that my soul has used to keep me under control. I will have a fresh mental and spiritual attitude and I will do what He's said. Amen.

Tasting The Truth

Are you really willing to do even greater things than Jesus did? What do you think that will be?

_____

_____

_____

What is it that you have to put off so that you can believe you can do this?

_____

_____

_____

What is our first assignment, our first job here (Ephesians 4:22-24)?

_____

_____

_____

_____

What do we need to discard?

_____

_____

Why?

_____

_____

_____

Wow, Lord, this is sounding serious. I will strip my soul of all of its preconceived ideas and half-truths and I will fill it with the whole truth of your Word. No more deception and denial for my soul. I want that fresh mental and spiritual attitude, and I want to put on the new nature. I want to start living as a new creature and enjoy all of your blessings and empowerment and all the other good things you said you would see that I had to do your will. I am excited to bind my will to your will and bind my mind to your mind. I can't wait. Amen.

3

Silver Basket

PRAYING
RIGHT PRAYERS

Golden Apple One

Praying In Agreement With Him

"Therefore I exhort first of all that supplications, prayers, intercessions, and giving of thanks be made for all men, for kings and all who are in authority, that we may lead a quiet and peaceable life in all godliness and reverence. For this is good and acceptable in the sight of God our Savior."

(1 Timothy 2:1-3, *NKJV*)

*P*rayer should not be an attempt to convince God to do what you think should be done. God does not need to be convinced to do what He knows needs to be done. But for some incredible reason unknown to us, He does want our agreement that His plans and purposes for any given situation are best.

Right prayers seek that God's will would be done on earth as in heaven, leaving all the details to God. Gorgeous, super-spiritual prayers are not always right prayers. Prayers that invoke Scripture to validate a personal agenda are not right prayers. Prayers of great petition and intercession for your idea of the best possible answers are not always right prayers.

Secondly, right prayers seek the best for everyone in a situation. Praying with a wrong attitude can backlash on you. Your old self (unsurrendered soul) does not want to pray with pure motives, but you can make it do it anyway. You can force your soul to surrender its wrong patterns of thinking and the wrong attitudes that go with them.

Jesus, I need your help to pray right prayers for the people and the situations I'm struggling with. I bind my will to the Father's will and I loose all wrong patterns of thinking that keeps me from wanting God's blessings for everyone who has been involved in the difficult times of my life. Thank you for helping me to overcome all of my wrong mindsets and attitudes. Amen.

Tasting The Truth

Prayer should never be an attempt to do what?

_____

_____

What does God want from us in prayer?

_____

_____

What do right prayers always seek first?

_____

_____

_____

What should right prayers seek secondly?

_____

_____

Name some of the wrong prayers that people pray.

_____

_____

Praying with a wrong attitude can backlash on you. What does that mean to you?

_____

_____

I want to pray right prayers. I want to agree with your precepts and principles, with your commandments. I want to be used to call your will into being here on earth. Lord, help me to recognize when I have not always prayed for your will to be done. I want to pray that way now. I want to be one you can count on to agree with you that your will is the best thing for everyone involved in all situations. I will pray. Amen.

Golden Apple Two

Prayer Changes The One Who Prays

"'My soul is overwhelmed with sorrow to the point of death,' he said to them. 'Stay here and keep watch.' Going a little farther, he fell to the ground and prayed that if possible the hour might pass from him. 'Abba, Father,' he said, 'everything is possible for you. Take this cup from me. Yet not what I will, but what you will' . . . Once more he went away and prayed the same thing . . . Returning the third time, he said to them, 'Are you still sleeping and resting? Enough! The hour has come . . . Let us go.'"

(Mark 14:33-42, *NIV*)

Jesus prayed His way through anguish and tears to a changed heart. He was completely human when He was facing impending death, and His soul did not want the cross. Knowing the will of the Father, however, He struggled in prayer to surrender His thoughts and feelings. Three times He went away from His friends to pray, asking if there was any other way.

I do not think the Son of God ever considered not obeying His Father, but I do believe He struggled in prayer to change His heart to be in agreement with God's will for Him. Jesus did not sin by asking the Father to take away the cross if there was any other way. He reconfirmed His obedience to God's will each time He asked. Finally, He broke through in prayer, accepted the coming cross and arose to go and meet the end of His life.

We often pray asking for others to change. The main reason to pray is to agree that God's will in heaven needs to be done on earth. The next most important thing our prayers accomplish is they change our attitudes and our motives.

Lord, I want your will done on earth. I also want your will done in me. I want to be changed. I want to pray without bias or personal desires. I want to pray with pure love. Amen.

Tasting The Truth

What did you learn from this Golden Apple? Can you use it to make a positive change in your life?

_____

_____

What did Jesus do to change His heart?

_____

_____

_____

Why do you think He had such a struggle?

_____

_____

_____

Was it wrong for Him to ask if there was another way? Explain your answer.

_____

_____

_____

Who should we be praying will change? Why?

_____

_____

_____

APPLES of GOLD
in BASKETS
of SILVER
Proverbs 25:11

I want to be changed and renewed in my prayer life. I want to pray pure prayers that are in agreement with your will and plans, Father. I want to be the one who will always agree with your will needing to be done. Lord, help me to realize that I must become changed. I will pray until I break through to change, as Jesus did. Thank you, Jesus, that you kept the Father's will ever in focus even though you were struggling with incredibly painful human feelings. Because of your obedience, I am now part of the family of God. Amen.

Golden Apple Three

Praying Focused Prayers (by L. Cady)

*"Do you not know that those who run in a race all run,
but only one receives the prize? Run in
such a way that you may win."*

(1 Corinthians 9:24, *NAS*)

*I*s it your desire to finish well, perhaps even win the prize, in the race of life? If your answer is yes, then you must determine where your focus is. True athletes cannot succeed without focusing on their training and their goals. They must focus on a desire to finish well.

Many Christians today are distracted and unfocused in many areas. Are your prayers focused on the Lord Jesus Christ? Are your prayers focused on agreeing with God that His will would be done on earth? Or are your prayers focused on what you fear Satan is doing? Whenever we spend time looking at the works of our enemy, we are giving him our focus.

Upon looking deep into my own soul, I have found myself spending too much time looking at the damage Satan has done or can do. That is time and opportunities lost. I have now determined to focus on the Word and the promises of God. There is never time or opportunities lost when I do this. A good way to focus your prayers is to pray His Word. Pray Psalm 23 this way, and then search the Word of God for more Scriptures to personalize in prayer.

Lord, you are my Shepherd who meets my every need. Thank you for making green pastures for me to lie down in with quiet waters to restore my soul. Help me slow down and recognize them every time you lead me to them. Because I am known by your name, I do not ever have to fear because I know you are with me. Your rod of correction and staff of protection are a comfort. Your goodness and loving kindness will follow me all of my days. Thank you, Lord. Amen.

Tasting The Truth

Why must you have focus in order to run the Christian race?

_____

_____

_____

Where do athletes have to place their focus?

_____

_____

In your prayers, are you spending more time praying for deliverance from Satan's works or are you thanking God for what He's done for you? Explain your answer.

_____

_____

_____

Whenever you focus on what you fear Satan may be doing to you and to your loved ones, what is lost? What else could you have been doing?

_____

_____

_____

Write a short prayer from another passage of Scripture here.

_____

_____

_____

I want to finish well, even win the prize. I don't want to run just to run. My focus will be on obeying the Lord so that I can do what He wants me to get done. I will resist distractions and I will resist Satan's attempt to get me unfocused. This is serious stuff, this praying for your will to be done. Amen.

Golden Apple Four

Praying Is An Open Door (by L. Cady)

"You are of God, little children, and have overcome them, because He who is in you is greater than he who is in the world."

(1 John 4:4, *NKJV*)

You have an open door to God the Father through Jesus Christ himself. He is the door to love, blessing, peace, and all perfect things. He is the door to success in every work you put your hand to this day, and He is the door of strength whenever you are feeling overcome. Paul told the Roman Christians that whatever their circumstances, they were *"more than conquerors through him"* (Romans 8:37, *KJV*). This promise is for you as well. No circumstance can overtake you unless you let it.

Perhaps you are struggling with family problems, money problems, or health problems. Just go to the door whose name is Christ Jesus and walk on through. Every time your mind, will, or emotions start to get out of alignment with the Word of God, repeat the verses above. Jesus in you is greater than any circumstance or trick of the devil.

You can overcome and conquer all circumstances because the Father loves you and will never forsake you. Guard your personal motives in wanting to help God bring His plans to pass. He does not need your help, He just wants you to agree that He knows best and then stay out of His way

Soul, you will bless the Lord today and you will eat of His Word today. The Word is alive and quick and able to cause change and life to flow into you—so receive it! Help me know, Jesus, when to reach out and embrace and enfold others who are struggling with the same things I was struggling with just minutes ago. I loose all efforts of my soul to withstand the healing power of your Spirit. Amen.

Tasting The Truth

What can you use in this Golden Apple to make a positive change in your life?

_____

_____

_____

How is Jesus a door to all perfect things?

_____

_____

_____

_____

Can you believe that He will help you be a conqueror? If not, why not?

_____

_____

_____

_____

Why should you guard your personal motives about trying to help God?

_____

_____

_____

Jesus told the Roman Christians they were more than conquerors through Him. What do you think that means?

_____

_____

I thank you for the door of prayer. I thank you for the door of healing. I thank you for Jesus Christ, who is the source of all that I need. Because He has conquered and won over death and hell, nothing can overtake Him. I thank you that I can go to Him any time I need strength and help. I bind my mind, will, and emotions to you, Jesus. I will stand steady. I will always remember and say that you are the greater one. Amen.

53

Golden Apple Five

Praying With Others

"Again, I tell you that if two of you on earth agree about anything you ask for, it will be done for you by my Father in heaven. For where two or three come together in my name, there am I with them."

(Matthew 18:19-20, *NIV*)

The Greek word translated as "gathered together: is *sunago* which comes from the Greek words *sun* meaning "together and completeness" and *ago* meaning "to lead, to draw, to bring into, or to induce." The two or three who are "*gathered together*" in His name (in verse 20 above) are people who have been drawn or led by His Spirit into togetherness and completeness with Jesus. Any prayer coming out of such agreement is going to be answered by the Father every time.

Praying in agreement with people who have been led or drawn together by any influence other than the Holy Spirit's can be both ineffective and potentially dangerous. This is why some prayers of agreement fail to manifest answers hoped for. This verse does not mean that any group praying together for the same thing will automatically receive the answer they are seeking.

Whenever you're not being led by the Holy Spirit to come together in agreement, you can convince yourself and others to agree on perfectly logical things that God is not any part of. It won't matter if you're praying in Jesus' name or not, a Matthew 18:19 response will come only to those "*gathered together*" by the Holy Spirit, as in Matthew 18:20. When God's Spirit gathers a group of people together to pray, they always pray the Father's will. He always answers those prayers.

Lord, I want to be drawn into prayer with others by your Holy Spirit. Help me to find people who are also drawn by your Spirit into praying in agreement so we can be fruitful. Amen.

Tasting The Truth

What does *sunago* mean?

_____

_____

Who needs to gather any prayer group? How does this happen?

_____

_____

_____

Praying in agreement with people not drawn together by the Spirit is what?

_____

_____

What must always be a part of praying together to ensure a Matthew 18:19-20 response?

_____

_____

_____

What does the group called by the Spirit always pray?

_____

_____

When will God always answer the prayers of a group who has come together to pray?

_____

_____

I want to be drawn by your Spirit to pray with other people. Lord, help me always discern the intents and motives behind others' prayers. I do not want to be exposed to soul ties. I want to pray in right agreement. I do not want to convince others or have others try to convince me to pray prayers that have nothing of God in them. Thank you, Lord, for allowing me to learn more about you and right prayer. Amen.

APPLES of GOLD
in BASKETS
of SILVER
Proverbs 25:11

55

Golden Apple Six

Don't Pray Soulish Prayers

"When you ask, you do not receive, because you ask with wrong motives, that you may spend what you get on your pleasures."

(James 4:3, *NIV*)

*R*ight prayers always seek that the will of God would be done. Soulish prayers generally seek your will's desires and wishes. We're all tempted at times to pray from our souls and will do so until our souls become healed and free from our unmet needs, unhealed hurts, and unresolved issues.

Too many people pray and tell God how He should straighten out others' failures. Too many come to God with prayer shopping lists. Too many come to God with prayers to change other people so they will come into alignment with the personal wishes and desires of the one praying.

Too many pray and ask God to cause things to happen that they think is best, such as praying for doctors to do a special surgery they have heard about. God may not want that surgery performed because He knows things about it that no human knows. We would all do well to guard against praying any prayers based upon personal or emotional feelings—ours or anyone else's.

A soulish prayer sounds good, feels good, and you think you know exactly how God should answer it. Praying soulish prayers in agreement with other believers can cause a soul-tie situation with them. Stop listening with your soul, stop agreeing out of your soul, and stop praying with a soulish agenda. The safest and most spiritual prayer you can ever pray is, "Not my will, but your will all the way, O God."

Lord, deliver me from praying soulish prayers. I will pray for your will only, I will thank you for performing it in your way and timing. Please, Father, forgive me and cancel out all soulish prayers I have prayed up until now. Amen.

Tasting The Truth

What is always the focus of any right prayer?

_____

_____

What are soulish prayers about?

_____

_____

What needs to happen before we stop praying soulish prayers?

_____

_____

What do some praying people do that that they shouldn't?

_____

_____

What do you need to guard against when praying with others?

_____

_____

_____

How can you identify a soulish prayer? What consequence can come from praying them with others?

_____

_____

_____

I will not pray soulish prayers any more. I will not tell God to straighten out other peoples' lives and problems anymore. I will bind myself to your will, Father, and I will bind them to your will as well. I don't want to pray any more ineffective prayers. I will stop listening to my soul and praying its ideas. I will pray for your will to be done, Lord. Amen.

Golden Apple Seven

Praying Pure Prayers

"So in everything, do to others what you would have them do to you, for this sums up the Law and the Prophets."

(Matthew 7:12, NIV)

When you are praying for others, think about how God would want you to pray for them and then think about what you would want them to pray for you. Here's a list of how you could pray for others like you wish they would pray for you.

Pray for God to use you as He see as necessary in order to bring your lost loved ones back to himself. Pray for those who have used you that God would bless them and heal them. Pray for God to shower His mercy and grace upon that coworker who has been so spiteful and ugly to you.

Pray and ask God to pour blessing and revelation into a spiritual leader you think is boring, binding him or her to God's will for their destiny. Pray and ask God to anoint the one chosen for that position in your church (instead of you), giving favor so that he or she would be successful.

Our perceptions of what would be right or wrong and what is needed are so narrow, and God's perception is so big. Understand that He knows best about what to do. To truly understand something means your perception of it has to come into line with God's reality of it. None of us are there all of the time, at least not yet. Agree that God that He knows all of the details (including many we do not), that He knows what is best for everyone involved. Pray that His will would be done for all.

Lord, I agree. You know so much about situations that I don't. I cannot believe I thought I knew the answers Your answers will consider the best for everyone. Mine don't. I ask you to make me more compassionate and kinder. Amen.

Tasting The Truth

When you are praying for others, what two things should you think about?

_____

_____

How could you should pray for someone who had used and abused you?

_____

_____

_____

How could you pray for a preacher you think is boring?

_____

_____

_____

How could you pray for someone who was chosen for a position in the church that you wanted to have?

_____

_____

What does it mean to truly understand something?

_____

_____

How can you pray best for yourself?

_____

_____

_____

APPLES of GOLD
in BASKETS
of SILVER
Proverbs 25:11

I want to pray right prayers for other people, too. I will ask you what you want, Lord, and I will think about what I would want prayed for me before I pray for anyone else. If I am praying for unsaved or backslidden loved ones, I will pray that God uses me however He wants. I want my perceptions in alignment with God's will. I want Him in charge. Amen.

Golden Apple Eight

Praying In The Midst Of The World

"As you sent me into the world, I have sent them into the world. For them I sanctify myself, that they too may be truly sanctified. My prayer is not for them alone. I pray also for those who will believe in me through their message."

(John 17:18-20, *NIV*)

Christians too often try to keep from being used by God in the middle of the world. They have even quit jobs trying to get out of the mainstream of daily life. What if most Christians in the body of Christ only worked at home or with other Christians? Who would show His love to the non-Christian workers?

On the other side, who would push the ease-seeking Christians to get out of their own comfort zones? Who would best expose self-righteous and soulish Christians, convicting them to change? It probably won't be the person next to you in your nice church. More likely it will be those "irritating" non-Christians who seem to always be pressing, rejecting, criticizing, and mocking "good Christians" who will push the hot buttons of comfort-zone Christians and set them off.

What if the unbelievers were to say out loud what many of them are probably thinking: "Hey, Christian! Show me that I'm wrong and you're right. Your T-shirts, posters, and Jesus coffee-cups haven't shown me anything! Prove to me that your God could love me, that He could really change my life!" Today pray and think and talk as if you believed every unbeliever was wishing you would show His love to them. Think about how you can have opportunities to let them even vent about your faith. Be wise in how to show them love.

I want to be used today, Lord, right out there in the middle of life with all of its messiness. Show me someone to speak to, someone to be kind to. Show me someone to love. Amen.

Tasting The Truth

Why do you think that some Christians go to quite a bit of trouble to get away from non-believers?

_____

_____

_____

Why do Christians need to stay in secular jobs?

_____

_____

Who is the one who can get to the Christian who needs a few hot buttons pushed?

_____

_____

_____

Can you ask God to give you opportunities to listen to non-believers' gripes about Christians? If not, then how should you pray for your attitude?

_____

_____

_____

Why do Christian T-shirts and coffee cups sometimes make non-believers so down on Christians? (Hint: it has to do with hypocrisy.)

_____

_____

APPLES of GOLD in BASKETS of SILVER
Proverbs 25:11

Lord, I want to be able to talk to non-Christians and make them feel they can say what they want. I will trust you to help me gradually bring the conversation around to how good you are and how much you love them. I loose the layers over my unhealed hurts so you can heal me so I won't react to what they might say. I want to be healed to be used. Amen.

Golden Apple Nine

Reality Checks On Your Prayers

"For my thoughts are not your thoughts, neither are your ways my ways, saith the LORD. For as the heavens are higher than the earth, so are my ways higher than your ways, and my thoughts than your thoughts."

(Isaiah 55:8-9, *KJV*)

We should all stop trying to help God fulfill our plans. He just wants us to agree with His plans, obey what He says to do, and then stay out of His way. All we know and understand, as if looking through a glass darkly, are the immutable attributes of God's character and the guidelines of His Word. We do not understand His ways of working out the daily details of our lives or the lives of those we are praying for.

His ways are not our ways and His thoughts are not our thoughts. If we get all caught up in struggling with why God isn't doing what we want, when we want, how we want, where we want it done, God probably isn't doing too much in our lives at all. Except, perhaps, keeping us breathing until we get tired of fussing and give up.

I have always struggled with drivers in front of me who do not seem to understand that green means go. I know that is pitiful and I apologize often to God for such an attitude. One day recently, as about ten cars in front of me sat as their drivers stared at the green traffic light, I suddenly realized that God might have a purpose in delaying me for a few seconds. It made me look at other delays in my life. Perhaps God has just been readjusting my time schedule to put me where He wants me when He wants me there—keeping me safe at the same time.

Holy Spirit, I think I really need to work on my spiritual fruit of patience. I ask you to do whatever you need to do to cause me to slow down and wait on God. Even at green lights. Amen.

Tasting The Truth

Instead of trying to help God, what should we do?

_____

_____

_____

When we are caught up in struggling with why God isn't doing what we want, what is the only thing He probably is doing?

_____

_____

_____

Why would God cause you to lose time sitting in a line of cars at a green light?

_____

_____

_____

Can you think of times when you have been mysteriously delayed in getting somewhere and found out that God was in it all the time? List those times and thank Him for doing it.

_____

_____

_____

Write Romans 8:28 here.

_____

_____

_____

APPLES of GOLD
in BASKETS
of SILVER
Proverbs 25:11

I want to pray reality prayers, Lord. I want to pray power prayers that get to the core issues in my life. Your will is the best prayer that can be prayed. I will stay out of your way. I will also remember that if I have bound myself to you, I should not worry about delays. Amen.

Golden Apple Ten

Praying With Love In Truth

*"Carry each other's burdens, and in this way
you will fulfill the law of Christ."*

(Galatians 6:2, NIV)

We never know whether any wounded lamb we meet is in great need of help, a jewel in hiding, or a future leader who is frustrated. In a meeting a few years ago, I noticed several very heavy women were first in line for prayer. I knew these women had suffered verbal abuse from Christians and non-Christians. As I was preparing to minister to the first woman, I heard the Holy Spirit say, *"Pray for each woman like you were praying for Miss America."* I knew these women had rarely been prayed for without hearing that God "would teach them new eating habits, deliver them from overeating, supernaturally cause weight loss so they could be used, etc."

I prayed for each woman that she would be anointed to take His Good News to ministers and church leaders, government leaders, and kings. I thanked God for their beauty, talents, faith, understanding, and value to His Kingdom. Hot tears flowed heavily in that line.

At times we have all wanted to encourage those who look like they could be winners. We haven't always been excited about praying for the one who is just too different. In our own finite thinking, we can miss the next Billy Graham or Kathryn Kuhlman. We don't know who might be holding back a ministry of miracles, just waiting for someone to confirm that he or she has something valuable to give. Be that voice of confirmation and encouragement. Be God's cheerleader!

Father, I want to pray for others as if I could not see or hear them, instead I could only hear you. I want to pray your prayers, not prayers about what I think the person needs. Anoint me to pray outside of my own mind and feelings. Amen.

Tasting The Truth

What are some ways we can carry each other's burdens (Galatians 6:2)?

_____

_____

_____

Why do we need to pray for the lovely and the unlovely exactly the same way?

_____

_____

_____

_____

We don't know who might be hold back a miracles ministry because of what reason?

_____

_____

_____

_____

The enemy tears down and discourages. Who can you pray for today that they would be encouraged?

_____

_____

Who will you call today and encourage?

_____

_____

APPLES of GOLD
in BASKETS
of SILVER
Proverbs 25:11

Today I want to reach out and touch those who tend to be overlooked. I want to be one who finds the hidden jewels, perhaps even the next miracle worker. I want to encourage those who feel like they could never win and cause them to realize they are loved by Him as much as He loves princes and princesses. Lord, help me become more sensitive and loving to everyone. Amen.

Silver Basket

SPIRIT OR SOUL?

Golden Apple One

Dividing Of Soul And Spirit

"For the word of God is living and active. Sharper than any double-edged sword, it penetrates even to dividing soul and spirit, joints and marrow; it judges the thoughts and attitudes of the heart. Nothing in all creation is hidden from God's sight. Everything is uncovered and laid bare before the eyes of him to whom we must give account."

(Hebrews 4:12-13, *NIV*)

God the Father has designed you to function with His power and blessings in a perfectly integrated body, soul, and spirit. Your body is designed to obey both your born-again spirit and your soul. When you are out of alignment with God's plans, your body just wants good food, sensory pleasures, comfort, and ease. If these are provided, your body will fall into line with whoever appears to be in charge of providing its wishes and desires.

Your spirit is that part of you that relates to God's Spirit and wants to be one with its Creator. Until your new birth, your spirit was an orphan with no connection to its Creator. Now it rejoices in its new position of being connected to the Father.

Your soul—mind, will, and emotions—is also meant to be in perfect alignment with God's will and purposes for your whole being. But it is not open to such an idea, wanting to be the final word on all decisions, overruling any input from your body, your spirit, God, or anyone else! As it plots to maintain its "kingdom," God understands the pain of every wrong thought, grudge, and wound it is trying to protect. It doesn't understand that He only wants it healed and set free.

Lord, I bind my soul to your will and purposes for it. I want it to receive your love, grace, and healing. I want my soul to want to be a part of your plans for my life. Help me! Amen.

Tasting The Truth

Because the Word of God can supernaturally cut between the differences of your soul and spirit, it is an important spiritual diagnostic tool for you. Can you name another Scripture that speak of the Word's supernatural ability in your life?

_____

_____

How do you think your unsurrendered soul tries to get your body into agreement with it to overwhelm your spirit?

_____

_____

_____

Hannah was so grieved over being barren, she wept bitterly in the House of the Lord. Matthew Henry believed she came to this conclusion in 1 Samuel 1:9: "Do I well to be angry? Do I well to fret? What good does it do me? Instead of binding the burden thus upon my shoulders, had I not better ease myself of it, and cast it upon the Lord by prayer?" What burdens have you bound to yourself that you need to cast upon the Lord by prayer?

_____

_____

_____

_____

Your soul wants to overrule input from who?

_____

_____

Lord, I need to get rid of the burdens that you have not meant for me to carry on my own shoulders. I cannot resolve them, I cannot change them, and I cannot fix them. But I can change my former patterns of dealing with them. I loose all of my disappointments, my frustrations, and my anger. I await your solutions and your grace and mercy. Thank you. Amen.

Golden Apple Two

Born Again Into His Kingdom

"'How can anyone,' said Nicodemus, 'be born who has already been born and grown up? You can't re-enter your mother's womb and be born again. What are you saying with this born-from-above talk?' Jesus said, 'You're not listening. Let me say it again! Unless a person submits to this original creation—the wind hovering over the water creation, the invisible moving the visible, a baptism into a new life—it's not possible to enter God's kingdom."

(John 3:4-5, *The Message*)

We are all born into this natural world with a functional human body and a blank soul. Whether our parents were Christians or not, our spirits were "off line" when we are born. Our spirits had no link to our Creator and had no function. Right away our souls began making self- focused choices for our lives.

To accept Christ, your soul had to be convinced to consider that since God is ruler of everything and cares about His creation—wouldn't it be a good idea to link up with His plans? Your soul had to be influenced in some manner to allow God to be able to pour His supernatural love into it to convince it to make Jesus Christ your Savior. From that point on, though, I think your soul said **oops(!)** and began to backpedal away from this whole "Lord and Master thing."

But your human spirit had connected with its Father's Spirit and it held on for dear life! Rejoice that your spirit refused to be disconnected by your turncoat soul after your salvation. Now the goal is to get your soul to surrender and connect.

What a plan you had for those of us who were lost and going astray. I'm so glad you saved me. I want to be able to tell others how they can be saved too. Show me how to do that in the best way possible. Amen.

Tasting The Truth

We are all born into this natural world with what two operational parts?

_____

_____

What was the condition of your spirit?

_____

_____

When did that condition change?

_____

_____

How is your spirit designed?

_____

_____

How is your soul supposed to function?

_____

_____

How does it choose to operate instead?

_____

_____

What does God want for your soul?

_____

_____

Lord, I'm glad that nothing in me is hidden from you, because sometimes I don't know what is going on inside of me. I know you designed me to function wondrously but my spirit, soul, and body sometimes seems to all be going in different directions at once. Help me get my troops together. Amen.

Golden Apple Three

Salvation For The Soul

"Work out—cultivate, carry out to the goal and fully complete—your own salvation with reverence and awe and trembling (self-distrust that is, with serious caution, tenderness of conscience, watchfulness against temptation; timidly shrinking from whatever might offend God and discredit the name of Christ)."

(Philippians 2:12, *Amplified*)

The word salvation means deliverance, preservation, and safety. Paul wrote to the Philippian Christians who had already experienced the salvation of their spirits, and he seemed to say they had not yet experienced the salvation of their souls. First Peter 1:9 says that *"you are receiving the goal of your faith, the salvation of your souls."*

Your being a Christian is fine with your soul as long as it does not have to change. Change always produces strong resistance from the soul. It will kick up all kinds of pressure and stir up all kinds of heat when you try to break from its status quo.

God will not make your soul agree to surrender and accept its completed "salvation" through the work of the Holy Spirit—you must. While you are not responsible for meeting your own needs, healing your own hurts, and resolving your own issues—you are responsible for rejecting your soul's control issues and bad attitudes. Philippians 2:12 above tells us this is a task we should undertake with extreme caution and a tender conscience. Don't allow your soul to sidetrack this goal.

Lord, help me surrender all of my soul to you. I choose to bind myself to you and to loose all of my soul's unforgiveness, anger, grudges, self-agendas, wrong intentions, and self-focused motives. I also loose all of its controlling attitudes. I want my soul set free and in safety with you. Amen.

Tasting The Truth

The salvation of your soul must be initiated by you, even though the Holy Spirit initiated your spirit's salvation. You must surrender the self-focus and carnal power your soul controls. Write a short prayer committed to loosing these things from your soul.

_____

_____

_____

_____

Peter implied above that the goal of your faith is to see the salvation of your soul. How will faith help you cooperate with this work of soul surrender?

_____

_____

_____

Have you tried to make changes before and had backlash from your soul? Write a brief prayer here for loosing your soul's denial, deception, and manipulative thoughts about change.

_____

_____

_____

You are not responsible for meeting your own needs, healing your own hurts, and resolving your own issues, but you are responsible for what?

_____

_____

I did not know I had a double agent in me—my own soul! Why would it reject and run from the love and blessing that the Father wants to impart to it? I'm not sure whether it is power mad or just fearful, but I loose all wrong ideas it has about controlling everything, and I loose its patterns of thinking that cause my emotions to flood with fear. Please heal my soul and fill it with grace and mercy. Thank you. Amen.

Golden Apple Four

Stop The Struggle

*"For we are God's workmanship, created in Christ Jesus to do good works,
which God prepared in advance for us to do."*

(Ephesians 2:10, *NIV*)

God has prepared great and mighty works in advance for us to do!
These works will cause us to be rejoicing when we are finally ready
to step into them. That is not going to require great strength and
spiritual power to overcome demons and evil people like you might think. It is
just going to require that you overcome your unsurrendered soul's deception
and fear.

Do you have an unsurrendered soul? If you struggle with any of the commands
of God's Word, with fear and doubt, with any authority over you, with any of
your family members, with any of your neighbors, with waiting for answers, if
you struggle with anything—you have an unsurrendered soul!

To show us when we're operating out of unsurrendered souls, God may bring
us into serious situations where we can't think our way out, emotionally
manipulate our way out, or "strong will" our way out. So few people recognize
that God allows us to get into these crises to break open the hard headed
attitudes of our souls. That hardness must be shattered to prevent it from
holding back the spiritual renewal that will allow us to move into our great and
good works for Him. Cooperation with God's principles both hastens and
graces that renewal process.

Do not be afraid when God gives you jump-starts to this renewal. This is His
way of getting you ready to move onward and upward to greater things.

*I'm ready to move on, God. Since I have trust and confidence in your goodness
towards me, I will not be anxious for anything. I will relax and be flexible in
your hands. Amen.*

Tasting The Truth

If you have been created to do good works, why aren't you doing them? You are probably not on the tracks of God's will. Write a short prayer to obligate and commit (bind) yourself to His will to bring you into closeness with those tracks.

_____

_____

_____

What do you struggle with? Authority, surrender, fear of man, doubt? List your struggles here and then stop and pray over each one, asking God to show you why they exist.

_____

_____

_____

What if your loved one had an addiction that was killing him and you helped arranged a family and friend intervention to confront him to stop destroying himself? Compare that to God arranging an intervention crisis in your life when He cannot get you to realize a self-destructive belief or behavior.

_____

_____

_____

What is God trying to do when He allows crisis in your life?

_____

_____

_____

_____

APPLES of GOLD in BASKETS of SILVER Proverbs 25:11

I want to see the trials and tribulations of my life in a new light, Lord. I want to recognize that they may be you working on an intervention on my soul. I bind myself to your will so that I am under obligation to your love. I am so grateful and happy that you care enough about me to pursue me. Amen.

Golden Apple Five

Casting Down Vain Imaginations

"And it come to pass, when he heareth the words of this curse, that he bless himself in his heart, saying, I shall have peace, though I walk in the imagination of mine heart . . . the anger of the LORD and his jealousy shall smoke against that man, and all the curses that are written in this book shall lie upon him."

(Deuteronomy 29:19-20, *KJV*)

The word imagination (original Hebrew) means an idea or a framework containing a self-concept of the mind. A lot of money can be made off the soul's unfulfilled desires and imaginations, but very little from the regenerated spirit which is a major reason the world doesn't to cater to it. Many Christians do not want to give up their soulish imaginations.

Second Corinthians 10:5 (*KJV*) tells us that we should be: *"Casting down imaginations, and every high thing that exalteth itself against the knowledge of God . . . ."* *Thayer's Greek/English Lexicon* says this means to throw down, demolish, and destroy, <u>with violence and force</u>, the barriers between you and your knowledge of God.

Our souls think their job description is to throw up arguments, reasonings, and logic—strongholds—against God's input to keep us focused on their pitiful store of knowledge. But we think with finite resources while His thoughts come from infinity and have no boundaries or end of wisdom. When you bind your mind to the mind of Christ and loose all vain imaginations from your soul, you begin to open up new territory to fill with His Word and His revelation knowledge that He's been wanting to give you.

I want all vain imaginations gone. I loose them all. Please show me how to cooperate with receiving more knowledge of you. I'm excited that you will help me to do so. Amen.

Tasting The Truth

Ask the Lord to show you if you have ignored the Spirit's warnings against saying in your heart that you have peace about things your soul wants to do. List any concerns you have here and then go to Him in prayer and ask for understanding.

_____

_____

_____

Do you think that you have given into the world's subtle calls to pleasure your soul? List whatever you feel could be distracting your time from seeking more knowledge of God.

_____

_____

What does casting down imaginations in 2 Corinthians 10:5 mean?

_____

_____

_____

Compare our thinking processes with God's thought processes.

_____

_____

Binding your mind to Christ's mind and loosing vain imaginations from your soul accomplishes what?

_____

_____

APPLES of GOLD
In BASKETS
of SILVER
Proverbs 25:11

I know that my soul has many imaginations that it fantasizes about. I do not want to waste time doing this, so I loose all soulish imaginations from myself. I want to make room to receive divine revelation and understanding. I want to think in alignment with the mind of Christ. Help me, Lord. Amen.

Golden Apple Six

Artificial Life Support System Of The Soul

*"<u>Forgetting what is behind</u> and straining toward what is ahead, I press on •
toward the goal to win the prize for which God has called me
heavenward in Christ Jesus."*

(Philippians 3:14, *NIV*)

Your unsurrendered soul keeps excellent records of everything that has ever been done to you, said to you, or taken away from you. It might try to let the memories of God times slip away; but when intense negative emotions are involved, those memories seem to get "engraved" on your soul. Unhealed memories of emotionally intense happenings of years ago can seem to hurt as much as they originally did. Your soul reinforces those memories every time it reruns and digs through them trying to figure out how to fix them.

Digging up the what and the who of your past is not the answer. God's healing grace has nothing to do with what happened or who is to blame. Divine grace simply requires that you disengage your soul's fixation on blame placing and let God fix everything. He has the grace and He wants to give it. What has been blocking His grace from your painful memories? You have not known how to forget like Paul forgot.

Paul's use of the word forgetting in the above Scripture means: stop nurturing, stop caring for, and stop watering and fertilizing those memories of what is behind you. It is your soul's own caretaking that keeps those memories alive and burning. Refuse to allow it to keep rerunning the feelings, the thoughts, and the pain from them and watch those memories dim.

I will loose my soul's recycling industry every time it tries to fire it up. I do not want to be forever tending a hot bed garden of pain and fear. Soul, I will not let you keep rerunning those memories. I choose to change and become free. Amen.

Tasting The Truth

Your soul keeps excellent records of what?

_____

_____

What happens to your memory banks when intense negative emotions are involved in things that have happened to you?

_____

_____

Do you know someone else who has said, "I can still feel the pain I felt as if it happened yesterday"? Write a short prayer to pray for that person that they will stop rerunning their pain.

_____

_____

Think of something that devastated you when you were younger, but it has changed today. Perhaps someone made fun of your red hair or your skinny body—today you love your hair and you are glad you are slender. Why should this help you believe that God can also take the sting out of other memories more painful?

_____

_____

_____

What has been blocking God's grace from your painful memories?

_____

_____

If Paul could forget the things which were behind him so he could press forward to the things before him, I can, too. Lord, I really want to do this. If I've been keeping my memories on life support, help me to pull the plug on them. Amen.

Golden Apple Seven

Training The Soul

"Solid food is for full-grown men, for those whose senses and mental faculties are trained by practice to discriminate and distinguish between what is morally good and noble and what is evil and contrary either to divine or human law."

(Hebrews 5:14, *Amplified*)

To discriminate and distinguish between good and evil is not always as easy as one thinks. Some evil today is a very pale shade of grey, almost but not quite white. You must have faith, trust and confidence in the goodness of God, and be practicing the Word so you can be led by His Spirit to make the right choices.

When we are found to be wanting in our faith, there is little else that is spiritually good in us. Jesus prayed for the Apostle Peter that his faith might not fail. He knew that if Peter's faith stayed strong, everything else about this formerly volatile apostle would stand firm. Faith is confidence and trust in the goodness, power, and wisdom of God towards you.

Everything you have been through can train you for greater purposes than you have ever thought. Your spirit looks into eternity and glories in this truth by faith. Your soul doesn't have any such long-range vision and you frequently have to bat it around with the Word of God and say, "Get down soul, I'm being trained! What I've been through did not kill me, so it has made me better. Soul, we're going to come out on the other side of every fiery trial purified like fine gold and translucent as the golden streets of heaven (see Revelation 21:21). Then Jesus Christ will be clearly seen in my life." We all need to want to be clear vessels that show His light to everyone we meet.

Lord, yes! I want to be a translucent vessel with Him shining through me. I don't want me dulling any part of that picture. So show me how to cooperate with being purified. Amen.

Tasting The Truth

What did this Golden Apple teach you? What has it encouraged you to do?

_____

_____

_____

Why did Jesus pray that Peter's faith would not fail instead of praying that Peter would not do something foolish or that he would not get into an argument with someone?

_____

_____

_____

Can you think of any hard consequences you are going through because of wrong choices you have made that you could now see God wanting you to use as a means of training your soul?

_____

_____

Can you think of things to compare to a translucent vessel with light in it? For example, what does light shining through a stained glass window do to the light?

_____

_____

Don't forget that sometimes you have to strong-arm your soul. What weapon is the best possible one to use to do that?

_____

_____

APPLES of GOLD
in BASKETS
of SILVER
Proverbs 25:11

Lord, I do not want to remain childish in my walk with you, I want to grow into the role of being a spiritual father or mother. I need to learn more about discerning and distinguishing between good and evil. I will keep practicing what your Word tells me to do to train me for that. Amen.

Golden Apple Eight

He Restores Our Souls

*"He makes me lie down in green pastures, he leads me
beside quiet waters, he restores my soul."*
(Psalm 23:2-3, *NIV*)

Our souls need to be restored by our Maker. Our minds, bombarded with the images and sounds of the world, need peace. Many of us have wills that are damaged from the constant pressure of making impossible decisions.

Our souls need to be restored by our Maker. But unsurrendered human souls will not willingly submit to restoration and renewal from their Creator. Though He will not run roughshod over our beleaguered minds and wills, His promise is that He will make us to lie down in green pastures beside quiet waters to rest in Him when we have no strength left in us.

Our souls need to be restored by our Maker. When we were born, our souls were blank slates waiting to be written upon. They became covered with the writings of too many who were neither surrendered to the will of God nor experienced in the art of shaping blank souls into His image. But fear not, God has promised this: *"If you will look to God and plead with the Almighty, if you are pure and upright, even now he will rouse himself on your behalf and restore you to your rightful place. Your beginnings will seem humble, so prosperous will your future be"* (Job 8:5-7, *NIV*).

He has always planned a rightful place for you. He has waited for you to come and ask Him for help so that you could be restored in your soul and made ready to take that rightful place. Place your trust in Him, for He will not disappoint that trust. Ask your Maker to begin to restore your soul even now.

Father God, I'm tired and my soul is raggedy. I come to you with my broken dreams and hopeless efforts. Please restore my soul and prepare me for the rightful place that you always planned would be mine in these days. Amen.

Tasting The Truth

What would it be like to come away from the craziness of the world and lie down in a green pasture beside quiet waters?

_____

_____

If your mind were restored to God's original plan for its operation, what do you think you might be able to think of?

_____

_____

Would you say your will has been hardened or has it been chipped away at, even broken, by the constant need to make difficult choices in today's world?

_____

_____

What could such a wonderful place be—your rightful place? Describe what your rightful place might be like.

_____

_____

He has waited for you to come and place your trust in Him. Trust and hope in Him will never disappoint you. If you could ask Him to do one thing for you and He would, what would that one thing be?

_____

_____

_____

Thank Him now for either giving you that one answer or for giving you something that He knows is better. You can trust Him to do one or the other

_____

_____

APPLES of GOLD
in BASKETS
of SILVER
Proverbs 25:11

Lord God, I choose to believe that you want to give good things to me, good things that are far above and beyond what I might ask for. I do thank you for what you are preparing for me even now as you are restoring my soul to receive it. Amen.

Golden Apple Nine

Holy Ghost Roadblocks

"Paul and his companions traveled throughout the region of Phrygia and Galatia, having been kept by the Holy Spirit from preaching the word in the province of Asia. When they came to the border of Mysia, they tried to enter Bithynia, but the Spirit of Jesus would not allow them to."

(Acts 16:6-7, *NIV*)

*P*aul and his friends were "roadblocked" by the Spirit from preaching the Gospel in Asia at that time. Only the Spirit knows why. Paul went instead to preach elsewhere, including a Roman colony at Philippi. Paul was fully obedient and did as he was directed. Others were sent to Asia later.

Both Satan and your soul will try to convince you that a roadblock of the Holy Spirit is really Satan's work to keep you from God's will. Many Christians have worn themselves out trying to get past one of the Holy Spirit's roadblocks, some even managing to do so to their own detriment. Authorities generally set up roadblocks to stop people from going into unsafe circumstances. I believe God does the same thing and if we ignore Him, we can land in a deep canyon!

God wants us to realize that He knows where we should not go, and that He does not want to just be the "tow truck" we call from down in the canyon. We must learn to check His Word and pray much when we are prevented from pursuing a path that we are sure is a directive from God. He will reveal the source of the roadblock. We are unable to recognize many of the works of God by our own natural thinking. Thank you, Jesus, for the Spirit of God who will lead us into all truth.

I'm really ready to stop calling you from the bottom of the canyons I've fallen into. Please teach me more about discerning roadblocks and their purposes. Amen.

Tasting The Truth

Name some reasons why God might prevent His ministers from ministering in a new area.

_____

_____

_____

The Romans were more despised by the Jewish leaders than other Gentiles. What might have God been planning when He sent Paul to the Roman colony instead of Asia?

_____

_____

Can you think of times in your life when you thought Satan was trying to stop you from God's will, but you found out that it was God blocking your way all the time? Did you learn anything from that?

_____

_____

_____

What are all good roadblocks supposed to accomplish?

_____

_____

How do we learn to recognize the sources of roadblocks?

_____

_____

I don't want any more canyon experiences while you are training me to be your end time messenger. I will not rely on my own finite thinking when I sense that something is not what it seems to be. I will bind my mind to the mind of Christ and force my soul to defer to the wisdom and counsel of the Holy Spirit. I will check the Word and I will pray much every time I am prevented from pursuing a good path. Amen.

Golden Apple Ten

God Will Not Be Fooled

"Do not be deceived and deluded and misled; God will not allow Himself to be sneered at—scorned, disdained or mocked by mere pretensions or professions, or His precepts being set aside. He inevitably deludes himself who attempts to delude God. For whatever a man sows . . . he will reap."

(Galatians 6:7, *Amplified*)

When your soul wants to avoid doing something, it will try to convince you that you really are acting on God's precepts when you are not. Or it will try to convince you that you can't do what God's Word says to do, quickly assuring you that God accepts this because of everything that has happened to you. None of these pretensions or professions are acceptable to God.

You spiritually fulfill God's precepts and principles by focusing your belief in three ways, already having done whatever practical things you know to do (i.e., praying, avoiding known temptations, reading God's Word, etc.).

Ask your **spirit** to keep affirming to your soul that God pays close attention to those He loves and you can do what God has said to do. Make your **soul** stop focusing on and worrying over your circumstances. Make your **body** conform to your belief in God's love. Put on a smile, stop looking worried, and get on with life.

Make your body and soul cooperate with your spirit as you walk out the commands of God. He loves it when you commit all of yourself to Him in this manner, just as Abraham did.

I love the idea of having all my own troops in unity instead of my body, soul, and spirit all going in different directions. I bind every part of myself to you, Lord, as my Master planner. Thank you, Jesus, for making it possible for me to do this. Amen.

Tasting The Truth

When your soul wants to avoid doing something, it will try to do what?

_____

_____

_____

_____

What practical things do you do first before getting down to some serious spiritual realignment with prayer?

_____

_____

_____

What do you ask your spirit to do?

_____

_____

_____

What do you make your soul do?

_____

_____

_____

What do you make your body do?

_____

_____

_____

APPLES of GOLD
in BASKETS
of SILVER
Proverbs 25:11

I will not listen to the lies that my soul tries to sell me when it doesn't want to act on God's precepts. I will do the practical things I know to do, and then I will ask my spirit to tell my soul we can do what God wants. I will make my soul stop focusing on the negative, and I will act and look like life is good! I will commit and obey, focusing my obedience in every way I know how. I will make my body and soul cooperate with my spirit just like Abraham did. I will walk out your commands as you have asked me to. Amen.

Silver Basket

GIVING THANKS IN TRIALS & TRIBULATIONS

Golden Apple One

The Message Of Trials

*"Remember your word to your servant, for you have given me hope.
My comfort in my suffering is this:
Your promise preserves my life."*

(Psalm 119:49-50, *NIV*)

When you are hurt or filled with discouragement and sadness, you must always remember you have a choice to either accept the pain or to reach out to Him for learning and healing. You can try to stuff the hurt down into the basement of your soul, pretend it isn't there, and hope it will disappear. Or, you can bring it out into the open, expose it to His light, ask Him to teach you by it, and let Him heal you from its effects.

The world says that we should avoid pain at all costs. Take an aspirin, get a tranquilizer, find a drink, take drugs—anything to avoid pain. God says if you will face your tests, trials, and tribulations head on, feel their weight and their message and then turn to His Word, you can overcome their burden. This requires a fierce soul inventory, fierce faith and fierce hope, holding tight to your faith which will never disappoint you. He will never disappoint you when you do your utmost to trust Him with fierce faith.

Sometimes trials are necessary to a Christian's training of the soul, just as a tooth extraction or minor surgery can bring about healing and wellness of body. But Christians go through far more trials and tribulations than they need to simply because they are fearful and fight the trial rather than trying to learn from it. Ask God to teach you how to learn from small trials so you can avoid bigger ones. You can trust Him.

Okay, enroll me in the Academy of Learning From Trials. I know that I frequently forget easy lessons. I want to become a strong warrior of faith who can be sent to set captives free. Amen.

Tasting The Truth

After reading this Golden Apple, what do you think the message is that God wants you to see in your trials?

_____

_____

_____

What are your two choices regarding what you should do with your pain or discouragement?

_____

_____

_____

What does God want you to do with your trials and tribulations?

_____

_____

This requires you to face them with what?

_____

_____

What can you compare the necessity of some trials to?

_____

_____

Why do some Christians go through far more trials than they have to?

_____

_____

I want to understand the message of my trials. Have I done something or made choices that have contributed to them? Have I ignored your Spirit, or are they lessons I just need to learn? I am ready to learn, God. I want to have your peace and joy and understanding. Amen.

Golden Apple Two

Controlled By The Spirit

"Walk and live habitually in the Holy Spirit—responsive to and controlled and guided by the Spirit; then you will certainly not gratify the cravings and desires of the flesh—of human nature without God."

(Galatians 5:16, *Amplified*)

Many are called, but few are chosen. You must lay down all of your own plans and desires in order to step forward to be chosen to fulfill a true calling of the Lord. Some not only don't step up surrendered and ready, they seem to deliberately eliminate themselves from His calling. But your Creator has purchased you for himself with the power of His own blood, and nothing has ever or will ever exist that has power over that blood. Know that He is very serious about successfully getting you into the middle of your purposes for living in these days.

God doesn't try to hide His precepts or make things difficult for us. He is not, as some feel at times, trying to run us through a maze after a piece of spiritual cheese. He has seen to it that everything we will ever need to know is in His Word for us to study and pray over. He has sent us the Counselor, His own Spirit, to give us understanding and guidance.

The unsurrendered soul will always be involved in a tug-of-war with the renewed spirit of its human being, as well as resisting the wooings of God's Holy Spirit. Jesus has left you the Keys of the Kingdom, however, keys to all the bars, gates, and padlocked doors, and you can rejoice as you use them to free yourself and come forth ready for your calling. Jesus knew you would need them and He wants you to use them.

Thank you for the keys you left for me. I'm sorry I have not used them enough yet. I am now ready to begin opening prison doors and padlocked gates. I'm really ready! Amen.

Tasting The Truth

You have been called to fulfill your destiny plans. If you have prepared and presented yourself truly surrendered and submitted to those plans and to God, your destiny will begin to unfold. Write here what this means to you.

_____

_____

_____

God is very serious about what regarding your purposes?

_____

_____

What do you believe is the main tug-of-war that your renewed spirit and your unsurrendered soul are having? Ask the Lord right now to reveal to you why you are allowing this to continue.

_____

_____

_____

God has seen to it that everything you need is where?

_____

_____

Write Him a thank you note here for sending you His own Spirit, the Counselor to give you understanding and guidance.

_____

_____

_____

Lord, what is going on inside of my soul that it is still trying to win this tug-of-war? How can I learn to surrender every time you ask me to? If I'm keeping my memories on life support, help me to pull the plug on them. Amen.

Golden Apple Three

Are You A Carrot, An Egg, Or A Coffee Bean?

"Consider it a sheer gift, friends, when tests and challenges come at you from all sides. You know that under pressure, your faith-life is forced into the open and shows its true colors. So don't try to get out of anything prematurely. Let it do its work so you become mature and well-developed, not deficient in any way."

(James 1:2-4, *The Message*)

*U*sing the analogy of a pot of boiling water as tests and tribulation, think about what happens to the carrot when it is immersed in boiling water. A very solid, firm vegetable becomes soft and squishy, but the water remains the same. An egg dropped into a boiling pot begins as a thin, fragile shell around a soft and silky interior. The boiling water soon hardens the inside of the egg, but the water remains unchanged.

A coffee bean dropped into boiling water releases its fragrance and its rich taste under the heat of its trial. It changes the boiling water into a strong, aromatic drink to warm the body and soul.

Hard times that come while you are doing your best to walk in righteousness are often an involuntary enrollment in God's hands-on courses in Kingdom living. Such times mean you probably have the mark of genuine greatness ahead of you in your Christian destiny. Just don't let your Kingdom training make you squishy soft or make you hard. Rather, let life here on earth cause you to release the fragrance and taste of Jesus Christ within you.

Jesus, if I need to be broken, crushed, tried, and even heated up to release the sweet fragrance of your presence within me, I give you permission to make it so. I will not fear such workings in my life because I can trust you in all things. Amen.

Tasting The Truth

Do you identify more with the carrot, the egg, or the coffee bean? Why?

_____

_____

_____

James 1:2-4 above says that under pressure, your faith-life is forced into the open. What does that mean to you?

_____

_____

_____

Write here how you might have changed your "boiling pot of water" in one of your recent trials if you had looked at it in a different light.

_____

_____

Write a short prayer here asking God to show you if your hard times are consequences of wrong choices, attacks of the enemy, or an advanced part of Kingdom living training.

_____

_____

_____

Enrollment in God's Kingdom living courses often mean that you have what?

_____

_____

I don't want to try to get out of your training sessions prematurely, Lord. I want to get through them with positive change in my life. I want to let everything you let come my way work a good work in me. I want to grow out of being immature, and I want to become well developed and ready to go wherever you assign me to go. Amen.

Golden Apple Four

There Must Be An Easier Way, Isn't There?

"I have learned in whatever state I am, to be content: I know how to be abased, and I know how to abound. Everywhere and in all things I have learned both to be full and to be hungry, both to abound and to suffer need. I can do all things through Christ who strengthens me."

(Philippians 4:11-13, *NKJV*)

When you are not quite sure yet how to be content while you are feeling abased, hungry, and needy, how can you tell the difference between Satan's slippery words and the Spirit's words? God will never condemn you or call you a loser or tell you it is hopeless. Whenever you hear those words, you are hearing the words of an enemy. Refuse to listen!

Bind yourself to God's timing and to the mind of Christ. Begin to loose the bondage thinking and other power tactics of your soul and choke off its complaining when things start nipping into your comfort zone. Loose the assignments of the enemy from yourself. When you remain secure in your faith regardless of your circumstances, people are going to be drawn to you because life and light will spark off you like you are under an arc welder.

Make your soul rejoice when tests just seem to keep coming even though you are doing your best to cooperate with God. Such intensity often means you are marked to become a mighty defender of the faith. It is easier to get through spiritual boot camp when you know that you are going to come out and be a spiritual general for God's people and God's plans when you graduate into the fullness of your destiny.

I'm ready to re-enlist in spiritual boot camp again, Lord. I'm still fussy with the whole abased and hungry and needy thing, but I don't want to be. I want to give off life and light to draw others to you. Amen.

Tasting The Truth

You learn to know the difference between words of Satan and words of the Spirit by learning the vocabulary of each. Satan's vocabulary is filled with urgings to complain and blame others. What are some of his other phrases?

_____

_____

What words fill the Spirit's vocabulary?

_____

_____

Write the opening lines of David's main praising prayer of insisting that his soul bless God.

_____

_____

_____

Loose bondage thinking from your soul and do what else?

_____

_____

Loose what of the enemy from yourself?

_____

_____

It's easier to get through spiritually hard times when you know what?

_____

_____

APPLES of GOLD
in BASKETS
of SILVER
Proverbs 25:11

Lord, give me understanding of how to look at tests and trials in the light of your Word. Help me to always remember to loose the assignments of the enemy from myself when I am struggling. I don't need to be carrying him on my back, too. I want to be trained well in your spiritual boot camp. Amen.

Golden Apple Five

Tests Come In Pleasing Packages, Too

"The crucible for silver and the furnace for gold, but man is tested by the praise he receives."

(Proverbs 27:21, *NIV*)

*I*n 1 Samuel 18:7-8, the men returned home after David had killed the Philistine giant, and women came out singing and dancing. This attention greatly pleased King Saul as he was not a secure man. But then he heard the women singing that Saul had slain his thousands, but David had slain tens of thousands.

This made Saul very angry and his thoughts became dark and jealous. He began to suspect David of wanting his kingdom next. This jealousy made Saul accessible by an evil spirit and he tried to kill David, but David got away. Then Saul let David marry his daughter, Michal, because he felt she could be used against hin. But David became even more successful.

Later after David became king, he brought the ark of the Lord to the City of David. Michal saw King David dancing before the Lord with all his might to celebrate and she despised him. She sarcastically accused David of being vulgar in front of the servants, and she became barren for the rest of her life.

Matthew Henry says that when men and women bind up their happiness in the praise and applause of men, they expose themselves to a perpetual uneasiness about every favorable word that is said of any other (Matthew 12:22-37). We must be on guard against this, for evil is always lurking to move in when jealousy of other's praise creeps into the heart. As one chosen of God, His praise of you is all you need.

I do not want to ever seek the praise of man, nor do I want to ever resent any praise of others. Lord, I want only your praise and your acceptance. I love you above all else. Amen.

Tasting The Truth

Those who are hungry for praise will often do unfortunate things in order to obtain it. Have you ever embarrassed yourself or compromised your standards in order to get the praise of man? Write a short prayer of repentance for this, asking God to show you how to let Him heal that need.

_____

_____

_____

Saul needed approval and respect. What shows that his daughter was like him in this way?

_____

_____

Have you experienced that uneasiness in yourself when favorable words were spoken about other people? Did you want to proclaim your good deeds, too?

_____

_____

_____

This neediness for praise and approval comes from deep unmet needs that have been in your soul for a long time. Stop now and pray, asking God to reveal this source to you and show you how He wants to heal it. Write down what He says.

_____

_____

_____

APPLES of GOLD
in BASKETS
of SILVER
Proverbs 25:11

I don't want to be needy anymore. You are more than sufficient to meet all my needs. I understand that I may have blocked you from doing so, but I want to change that. I bind myself to your will, obligating myself to you. I loose all the strongholds and defensive mechanisms that my soul has employed to keep you from healing me. Have your way with me. Amen.

Golden Apple Six

Trials From Satan And Your Soul

"Those on the rock are the ones who receive the word with joy when they hear it, but they have no root. They believe for a while, but in the time of testing they fall away."

(Luke 8:13, *NIV*)

In this parable, the heart is the planting soil where the seed of God's Word is sown. The success of the planting of this seed of the Word is highly dependent upon the condition of the soil. There must always be a cooperation by the heart of man with the spiritual things of God or new life's growth can be aborted.

The parable in Luke 8:4-21 tells of the Word of God being sown into four different kinds of heart conditions. The devil does not want these hearts to hear and believe the seed of the Word, because if they believe they might become saved. One heart condition here is said to have no depth to its soil and the seed of the Word was not able to gain any root in that heart.

Hebrews 2:1 says that *"we must pay more careful attention, therefore, to what we have heard, so that we do not drift away."* When we do not pay close attention to the Word, it does not root down within us. Then Satan and even our own unsurrendered souls will try to divert us from focusing on it.

Some seem to grab hold of the seed, but when trials come because of the Word—ridicule, teasing, disapproval—many let go of it and try to rescue their pride. The heart with the condition of good ground is one that is ready to receive instruction from the Word because that heart recognizes the precious value of the seed message.

Forgive me, Jesus, for being careless with God's precious Word. I know I have not paid close attention to it like I should. I want it to root down within me and produce fruit. Amen.

Tasting The Truth

How is the condition of the soil of your soul/heart? Is it deep enough, has it been harrowed or plowed enough? Sometimes trials and testings are really tractors for the soul. How do you relate to that?

_____

_____

_____

There must be a cooperation by the heart of man with the spiritual sowing of God's new life or what happens?

_____

_____

How do you think your soul tries to keep you from deep plantings and rooting of the Word?

_____

_____

_____

How do ridicule and disapproval relate to pride?

_____

_____

Do you think that your pride has caused you to let go of certain godly beliefs? How?

_____

_____

_____

APPLES of GOLD
in BASKETS
of SILVER
Proverbs 25:11

I know that I'm holy dirt for the planting of the Incorruptible Seed and the seed of the Word of God. Please teach me what I can do to plow up the soil of my heart. I want to be fertile soil, soil good for growing strong things. I will water that soil with my tears and prayers. I loose all of the tares and weeds from the soil of my heart. I loose all of the hard things that would interfere with life growing there. Help me, Lord. Amen.

Golden Apple Seven

Suffering And Trials Produce Character And Hope

*"We also rejoice in our sufferings, because we know that suffering
produces perseverance; perseverance, character;
and character, hope, and hope does not disappoint us,
because God has poured out his love into our hearts
by the Holy Spirit, whom he has given us."*

(Romans 5:3-5, *NIV*)

We are to rejoice in our sufferings because they are the experiences that produce perseverance in us. Being comfortable never produces follow-through and persistence. Perseverance is the ability to endure, to keep pressing forward when confronted by opposition or difficulty, to persist towards a goal or purpose. Such persevering produces character.

One with a good character is described as having been proven, being reliable and trustworthy, and having good moral fiber. One with good character always acts with integrity, a word that comes from the word integrate. When you have integrity, your behaviors and actions always integrate perfectly with what you say you believe about Christ. Integrity will always produce a direct correspondence between your words and your deeds.

Hope is favorable and confident expectation, a happy anticipation of good to come, a comfort when enduring a trial. Hope is also the anchor of your soul, securing you when you are being tossed about by the storms of life. Hope in God will never shame or disappoint the believer whose heart has embraced the love which the Holy Ghost gives freely to those who believe. Never be afraid to hope in Him, for He loves you and He always wants the best for you.

Lord, I need perseverance and character in my soul. If this takes tribulation to work this out in me, then I will rejoice in trials that come my way. I will always hope in you. Amen.

Tasting The Truth

Everyone in life goes through tribulation and hard times—good and evil people. What blessings come out of those hard times to the people of God?

_____

_____

_____

Those who are practicing evil hate hard times, rarely learning from them. Would you say this is true or false? Why?

_____

_____

_____

Being comfortable never produces follow-through and persistence. What do you think this means?

_____

_____

_____

How do you think that perseverance produces character?

_____

_____

When you have integrity, what happens in your life?

_____

_____

Please help me to learn perseverance to keep pressing forward towards the goals and purposes you set for me. Let that perseverance create good character and integrity in me. Then I will always have hope that nevers disappoints. Amen.

Golden Apple Eight

Rejoice In All Trials And Testings

"Consider it pure joy, my brothers, whenever you face trials of many kinds, because you know that the testing of your faith develops perseverance. Perseverance must finish its work so that you may be mature and complete, not lacking anything."

(James 1:2-4, *NIV*)

*P*aul, James, and Peter all encouraged believers to develop perseverance. Paul urged the Ephesian believers to be *"Praying always with all prayer and supplication in the Spirit, and watching thereunto with all perseverance and supplication for all saints"* (Ephesians 6;18, *KJV*). He told the Hebrew believers to run with perseverance the race set before them.

Endurance or patience is described in the original Greek language as having fortitude, being constant, and being able to endure. This makes patience sound somewhat more aggressive than passive as it sometimes seems. Aggressive faith always acts. Aggressive prayer always believes. Aggressive hope fiercely expects. Aggressive plans for destiny purposes look into the future anticipating the outcome. I like aggressive things of the believers' faith as found in the Word.

Peter said, *"Make every effort to add to your faith goodness; and to goodness, knowledge; and to knowledge, self-control; and to self-control, perseverance; and to perseverance, godliness; and to godliness, brotherly kindness; and to brotherly kindness, love. For if you possess these qualities in increasing measure, they will keep you from being ineffective and unproductive in your knowledge of our Lord Jesus Christ"* (2 Peter 1:5-8, *NIV*). Make us effective and productive, Lord!

Lord, I want the whole list. I am asking for all of the things on this list, and I am trusting you to help me grow into them. I will endure and persevere until I gain each one in full. Amen.

Tasting The Truth

Look up the words fortitude and constancy and write their meanings here.

_____

_____

When perseverance finishes its work, you will be what?

_____

_____

Give an example of aggressive patience.

_____

_____

Give an example of aggressive faith.

_____

_____

Give an example of aggressive hope.

_____

_____

We are to pray always watching thereunto with all perseverance and supplications for all saints. Write a commitment here that you will do this for the next seven days.

_____

_____

_____

I want to be mature and complete so that I am not lacking any part of you that I need within my soul. I want to begin praying and caring about others with perseverance. I want to follow through with hope that is aggressive. I want to fiercely expect God to move on my behalf and those I pray for. Amen.

Golden Apple Nine

Tribulation And Suffering Teach Obedience

"Although he was a son, he learned obedience from what he suffered and,
once made perfect, he became the source of eternal salvation
for all who obey him."

(Hebrews 5:8-9, *NIV*)

You may be despairing of so many devotions on trials and tribulations by now. Please don't. So much can be learned from the experience of coming through such trials rejoicing in newfound strength and faith. Jesus, our High Priest, rejoiced in all that He went through because of the reward He knew was going to be His one day. We have a great reward, too.

Hebrews 5:2 tells us that God chose high priests who had to care for, intercede for, and instruct those who were guilty of sins of ignorance. His high priests also had to deal with those who were going astray and not walking in truth, leading them into the right way with great compassion. The high priest's own weaknesses and infirmities gave him cause to sympathize with man's weak condition.

Our High Priest, Christ, is certainly able to love and instruct those who do not understand God's ways. As the mighty Shepherd, He also has a great heart for lost ones going astray, especially evidenced when He said how much rejoicing there would be over the one sheep found. He took upon himself all of our infirmities and lived with the frailties of the human condition. No high priest ever suffered as much for his calling or had to obey as many difficult things as Jesus did. What love, what hope He had for those who would be His bride some day. Thank you, Lord, for caring for me like that.

I am overwhelmed with wonder at why you would want us so much, Jesus. We are like sheep, all smelly, woolly, silly, and unable to stay where we are supposed to be. Thank you. Amen.

Tasting The Truth

Pray now and ask God to give you understanding of the strengths that only come from completing a trial and letting it have it full work in you. Write down what He says.

_____

What are some of the characteristics that God said His high priests must have?

_____
_____

No high priest ever suffered as much as Christ did for His calling. Write Him a thank you note here for His great love.

_____
_____
_____

What did the high priest's own weaknesses cause in him?

_____
_____
_____

What parallel do you think Jesus was drawing when He spoke of the rejoicing over the one lost sheep found?

_____
_____

APPLES of GOLD in BASKETS of SILVER Proverbs 25:11

I am humbled over what you endured as my High Priest. Your thoughts truly are higher than mine, and your ways higher than mine. Thank you for paying such a price for me, thank you. Help me to learn how to become more like you. I don't have a shepherd's heart, but I would like a heart more like yours. Amen.

Golden Apple Ten

You're Not The Only One

*"Dear friends, do not be surprised at the painful trial you are
suffering, as though something strange
were happening to you."*

(1 Peter 4:12-14, *NIV*)

Sometimes we have a tendency to feel that we are the only ones who go through difficult times in our Christian walks. We can become afflicted with tunnel vision, seeing only what concerns us. We need to always look out beyond our own situations and see what Jesus is doing to bring hope to other lives.

I have a friend who became consumed with the woes of his own life at an early age. He was angry and unforgiving about his childhood and his family's difficult relationship dynamics. One day I said that that his brother seemed to have had an even harder time of growing up than my friend. This man was blind to the experiences of his brother, saying, "I don't care what happened to him. I only care about what happened to me."

This is not a particularly unusual reaction to unhealed hurts and unresolved issues that are still scorching the life of an adult because of the unsurrendered soul's artificial life-support system. But it is very sad when a talented, successful, and highly intelligent adult with power to choose a new attitude and way of living his life cannot break out of the mold that was cast in his soul when he was so young. We can break free of old bondages and live as new creatures. Consider now if you are packing any chains from your past. You can begin to change today and see Him bring a new freedom and sweetness to your life.

I choose to break the shackles and chains from my soul. I cannot afford to drag them with me any longer. I will break the old molds of my past and set everyone, even me, free. Amen.

Tasting The Truth

What did you learn from this Golden Apple?

_____

_____

_____

_____

Are there areas of your life where you see things with tunnel vision?

_____

_____

_____

Have you ever walked past a hurting person and looked away so they could not meet your eyes because you were too focused on your own feelings and pain? Write a prayer of repentance and commit to God that you will reject such tunnel vision.

_____

_____

_____

List the pros and cons of continually rehearsing your hurts as compared to being free from them. Ask the Father to help you turn loose of them.

_____

_____

_____

Yes, Lord, I have ignored hurting people because I was too focused on my own pain. I don't want to ever do that again. Forgive me. Please touch those people now and meet their needs and show them your love. I do not want to pack any more chains from my past. I have the right and the ability to choose a new attitude and a new outlook and I choose to do that now. I will break the mold that was cast for me when I was young. It doesn't fit now. Amen.

6

Silver Basket

RECEIVING &
GIVING BLESSINGS

Golden Apple One

What Does It Mean To Bless Someone?

"Moses inspected the work and saw that they had done it just as the LORD had commanded. So Moses blessed them."

(Exodus 39:43, *NIV*)

Moses prayed to God in their behalf that these Israelite workers might be prospered in all their undertakings, saved from every evil, and brought to their inheritance from God that would never fade away. This is a fine blessing, even today. To bless, as used in both the Old and New Testaments, means to speak well of someone, to bestow a benefit, to invoke (call forth, bring into being) a benediction upon someone, or to prosper someone. Could this mean that we can actually call forth blessings upon others? I think it does.

Our mouths have the power to speak life and to speak death, to speak blessings and to speak curses. It is usually very easy to tell the condition of peoples' hearts (souls) by the words that come out of their mouths. The heart and the mouth are closely linked one to another. Proverbs 4:23 tells us how important it is to keep our hearts clean and pure. *"Keep your heart with all diligence, for out of it spring the issues of life"* (*NKJV*). This is saying that life or death actually comes forth out of our hearts.

What the world needs now, in addition to more love, is encouragement . . . sweet encouragement. One of Satan's most devastating tools is discouragement. When he can get us to lose heart, then he has us whipped. Bless and encourage those you meet up with <u>today</u>—not sometime later. Do your best now, as later doesn't always come for everyone. Encourage life to thrive and flow out to others from your heart.

For those who do well for me, and for those who don't, I will speak blessings upon them. I will invoke a benefit upon them by the words of my mouth. Amen.

Tasting The Truth

List the things that describe blessing. Would you be uncomfortable speaking those things to people in person? Why?

_____

_____

_____

Our mouths have the power to do what?

_____

_____

_____

How can you tell the condition of peoples' hearts?

_____

_____

People need encouragement today. See if you can encourage five people today. Then write here what their responses were.

_____

_____

_____

Write a prayer of commitment to stop using the word "later" and do what you can to bless and encourage others NOW.

_____

_____

_____

APPLES of GOLD in BASKETS of SILVER
Proverbs 25:11

I want to be a blessing and an encourager. I bind my will to your will, Father, and I commit myself to watching my words more carefully. I will remember that my words are revealing the very condition of my heart to everyone who hears me speak. I will set my will to do what you want now, not later. Amen.

Golden Apple Two

Blessing Follows Obedience

"Behold, I set before you today a blessing and a curse: the blessing, if you obey the commandments of the LORD your God which I command you today; and the curse, if you do not obey the commandments of the LORD your God."

(Deuteronomy 11:26-28, (*NKJV*)

This verse is not saying that God is going to put a curse on people who do not obey Him. They are cursed because they do not have His blessing. If you got wet in a rainstorm, I would not have made it rain on you. But you might be wet because I chose not to hold my umbrella over you.

Obedience to God's Word and His will is both opportunity and obligation. The opportunity is that all good things issue forth from every act of obeying. The obligation is that our Father has not commanded us to save ourselves, to heal ourselves, or to fix our world—He only commands us to obey His precepts that position us to receive all good things from Him.

We have learned to view obedience to anything other than our own desires and wishes as a bad thing. Our souls only want to do what they can think of or choose. The choice to do that is always there, and the consequences can be bad. God has plans for our good. We should thank Him for those plans to bless us, keep us safe, and deliver us from evil by obeying Him

Our motive for obeying should never be for the rewards, but for love. Still, God always rewards obedience. His Word promises this and He keeps His promises.

Jesus said that all of the commandments were summed up in loving our God with all our hearts and loving others. I will start there, loving Him abundantly and loving others. I will never consider my obedience to be a duty. Amen.

Tasting The Truth

Obedience to God's Word and His will is both opportunity and obligation. Write down in your words what you think that means.

_____

_____

_____

_____

Do you believe you can invoke blessing upon another person by the words of your mouth? If so, go out and bless three people today—whether you think they deserve the blessing or not. Write down their responses after you do.

_____

_____

_____

What should our motive be for obeying?

_____

What is our obligation of obedience?

_____

_____

_____

Do you think your motives for obeying God's Word are always right? Why not?

_____

_____

I want to look at obedience as an opportunity to show my love to you and an obligation of love for you. You have made my part in our covenant so simple. You do all the heavy lifting, I just have to listen and obey. Show me who to bless, show me who you want to hear a kind word today. Show me who is discouraged and about to give up. I will tell them of a God who is good and kind and loving and wants to help them. Amen.

115

Golden Apple Three

Blessing Upon Blessing

"I will make you a great nation; I will bless you and make your name great; and you shall be a blessing . . . and in you all the families of the earth shall be blessed."

(Genesis 12:2-3, *NKJV*)

In the Old Testament, God said He would bless Abraham and his family, make him a blessing, and bless all who blessed him. Through him, all the families of the earth would ultimately be blessed. Abraham's descendant, Jesus Christ, was the One who would bring salvation and blessing to anyone who would choose to receive it.

Now that's blessing mathematics that all people should want to be part of! Not everyone in God's family today is a blessing to other families on this earth. How can we learn and then teach others that our spiritual calling is to simply obey God and bless and love others? Being a great evangelist, a fiery preacher, a prolific author, or anyone who is fulfilling the Great Commission should flow out of this basic call on our lives. Why are we not fulfilling this simple directive effectively?

It surely has something to do with self-focus. When we are focused on our own perceived lack of blessings and feeling unloved, we are not positioned to receive the blessings and love we so crave. A candle loses none of its own light when it lights another candle. Its ray of light is added to and strengthened by the new source of light it has initiated. You are filled with the light of the world. You will lose nothing by sharing it, rather you will increase the light in the world. Let that light shine!

The world needs more light and love. Forgive me, Lord, for not remembering that I have an infinite source of both within myself. I will overcome my self-focus and give His light and love away to others who are in darkness and loneliness. Amen.

Tasting The Truth

Why do you think that Christians have moved away from Abraham's blessing patterns?

_____

_____

_____

How do you think you could help others learn how to be a blessing?

_____

_____

_____

What is our spiritual calling in its simplest form?

_____

_____

Why do you think everyone in God's family is not doing that?

_____

_____

_____

What can be done to change the attitudes of hurting people?

_____

_____

How can you relate your own life to the candle example?

_____

_____

APPLES of GOLD in BASKETS of SILVER
Proverbs 25:11

Please help me to be a part of continuing Abraham's blessing. I want to do that because I I love being a part of the fulfillment of God's promises. I am honored to be a part of anything He's doing. I also want to learn how to teach others that our spiritual calling is to simply obey God and bless and love others. Holy Spirit, teach me how to do this. Amen.

Golden Apple Four

Blessing Guaranteed To The Righteous

*"Let all who take refuge in you be glad; let them ever sing for joy. Spread
your protection over them, that those who love your name
may rejoice in you . . . you bless the righteous; you surround them
with your favor as with a shield."*

(Psalm 5:11-12, *NIV*)

*I*n Deuteronomy 28:2-10, we can read of the protection and
blessings God gave to His righteous people. Because we have
become His people, these blessings are promises to us, too. These
blessings shall <u>overtake</u> (isn't that a great word?) you if you obey the Lord your
God. You shall be blessed in the city and in the country. Your children, the
work of your hands, your possessions shall be blessed. You shall be blessed
coming in and going out and your enemies shall run away from you.

If you obey your God, all other people shall know you are called by His name
and will be afraid of harming you. You will always have plenty. God will open
up His good treasures, even the heavens, and give you rain to bless the work
of your hands. You shall lend to many, but never have to borrow. The Lord will
make you the head and never the tail who follows. He will make you the top
and not the bottom. He will just bless you and bless you and bless you.

His commands and requests are not that hard to follow, only your soul is
convinced that they are. Some of His commands are so simple, they are like
obeying a stop sign so you do not get hit by another car. His commands are
practical and realistic and filled with promise.

*This is an incredible list of promises to your people, Lord. I am yours and I do
desire to obey you because I love you. I want to obey your smallest command and
please you. How wonderful it is that my love can result in such blessings. Amen.*

Tasting The Truth

Your Lord is your refuge and He is your protection. He surrounds you with favor as with a shield Write God a thank you letter right here for such wonderful promises.

_____

_____

_____

_____

To hear that blessings will overtake the one who obeys God is incredible. Do you think God is saying here that when you obey Him, you will not be able to outrun His blessings?

_____

_____

_____

Which one of the blessings listed would most bless you? Write it here.

_____

_____

Why do you think the soul disbelieves the simplicity of obeying God?

_____

_____

_____

Some of His commands are so simple, they are like:

_____

_____

I am so glad that you will always be my refuge, that you are my protection. I rejoice in the truth that you surround me with your favor like a shield. Your commands are practical, yet filled with supernatural promises. All I have to do is obey you and love you and others. I am so blessed to do that. Amen.

Golden Apple Five

Being A Blessing To Others

"The LORD said to Moses, Tell Aaron and his sons, 'This is how you are to bless the Israelites. Say to them: The LORD bless you and keep you; the LORD make his face shine upon you and be gracious to you; the LORD turn his face toward you and give you peace.'"

(Numbers 6:22-26, *NIV*)

Verbally blessing someone is awkward to many. I've asked people in prayer meetings to bless the person next to them, and most of them only know how to pray. Prayers are always good, but let's learn how to invoke a blessing on someone in person. We are not really a nation that teaches people how to bless others. The Jewish people of the Bible were always taught about blessing their children and their loves ones and their friends. Choose to begin to practice blessing others today.

- At home, tell your spouse, "May the Lord make His face to shine upon you and be gracious to you today."
- Wherever, tell your children, "Bless you, my children, may God keep you safe and help you today."
- At work, tell a co-worker, "I bless you today and ask God to give you great favor with everyone."
- At your church, tell a stranger, "May the Lord look upon you and give you great peace today."
- At the store, tell a customer "May the Lord bless you and keep you safe and prosperous today."
- At the bank, tell an employee, "I bless you in everything you do today."

Lord, help me to be a blessing to someone, even many, today. Help me to come out of my focus on my life, my problems, my issues, and my needs. Bring people across my path today who need to hear a word of blessing, who need a word of kindness. I will invoke a blessing upon them in your name. Amen.

Tasting The Truth

Is praying for people the same as pronouncing a blessing upon them? Please explain your answer.

_____

_____

_____

How could you verbally bless one of your parents or another older relative of yours?

_____

_____

_____

How could you verbally bless a total stranger on the street?

_____

_____

What would you do if someone rejected your speaking a blessing to them? What do you think you should do?

_____

_____

_____

Call three people today to bless them. Write down their responses or prayer needs here.

_____

_____

APPLES of GOLD
in BASKETS
of SILVER
Proverbs 25:11

I want to become so comfortable in blessing others verbally that I won't be able to wait until I can do it again. I want to begin changing the fact that we are not a nation that teaches people how to bless others. I want to become an example for others to follow. I want to practice this attribute of my Father's. Please, Holy Spirit, show me how to bless even the unlovable and seeming unblessable. Amen.

Golden Apple Six

Words Can Bless or Hurt

"For out of the abundance of the heart the mouth speaks. A good man out of the good treasure of his heart brings forth good things, and an evil man out of the evil treasure brings forth evil things. But I say to you that for every idle word men may speak, they will give account of it in the day of judgment. For by your words you will be justified, and by your words you will be condemned."

(Matthew 12:34-37, *NKJV*)

It is a serious thing when a Christian speaks harsh and evil words. There is no justification to support any believers' right to tear down or debase any other human being. Anger is never a reasonable or right excuse for hard words. *"If any man among you seem to be religious, and bridleth not his tongue, but deceiveth his own heart, this man's religion is vain"* (James 1:26, *KJV*).

James' use of the word religion here is in direct contrast with *"pure religion undefiled before God"* which he describes in the very next verse. James is comparing an external show or display of religion to an internal state of a humbled heart.

Those practicing only an external form of religion rarely bless others except for personal gain. Rather, they tend to criticize and judge others. The heart of a man or woman can easily be read like a book by listening to the words that come from their mouths. Listen carefully to your own words, both those spoken and those secretly thought, for they will tell you the condition of your own heart.

I am ashamed of how careless I have been with my thoughts and the words of my mouth, Jesus. Forgive me and cleanse me, as well as those I have spoken ill of, from the stain of my careless and hard words. Help me to speak only life and blessing that my own words would not condemn me before you. Amen.

Tasting The Truth

Out of the abundance of the heart the mouth speaks. What does this mean?

_____

_____

_____

_____

By your words you will be justified and by your words you will be condemned.
Explain what this means.

_____

_____

_____

Compare an external show of religion to an internal state of a humbled heart.

_____

_____

_____

_____

Anger is never an excuse for what?

_____

_____

Those who practice only an external form of religion tend to exhibit what traits?

_____

_____

APPLES OF GOLD
in BASKETS
of SILVER
Proverbs 25:11

_I want the treasure of my heart to be good and holy. I do not want to
have idle words come back on me on the day of judgment, nor do I
want those same idle words to hurt anyone now. Please help me to
change my way of speaking. I want to uplift people, not make them
uneasy. I want to make them comfortable, instead of teasing and
jesting with them. I want to change, Lord. Amen._

Golden Apple Seven

Blessing Your Enemies

"Ye have heard that it hath been said, 'Thou shalt love thy neighbour, and hate thine enemy.' But I say unto you, Love your enemies, bless them that curse you, do good to them that hate you, and pray for them which despitefully use you, and persecute you."

(Matthew 5:43-44, *KJV*)

eople who are difficult or critical of you are not necessarily your enemies. They are human beings acting all too human. Sometimes critical people expose liabilities in your life that could ultimately humiliate you or cause you to fail—faults you have denied. Do not judge peoples' motives harshly lest you be judged harshly yourself. True enemies want to destroy your character, reputation, your loved ones, and even your life.

How do you bless someone who has cursed you? Find some way to speak well of them. Extend grace and the benefit of the doubt to them as you have opportunity to do so. How do you bless those who hate you? Pray and bind their wills to the will of God and their minds to the mind of Christ. Loose hurtful thought patterns and wrong mindsets from their souls. How do you bless those who have despitefully used and persecuted you? Forgive them and ask God to forgive them and heal them.

To test your own forgiveness, ask God to use you to bring blessing and healing to them. Do not rush into their lives, but give "so-called" enemies the room they need to learn to trust your motives. Just keep seeking their blessing through right prayer, speaking well of them, and showing love.

To love my enemies is a goal I will begin to work towards this day. Please bring everyone I've ever called or thought of as an enemy to my mind. I will forgive them, pray for them, speak well of them, loose word curses from them, and watch for opportunities to bless them. Amen.

Tasting The Truth

Who are your real enemies?

_____

_____

_____

How can a critical person benefit you?

_____

_____

_____

How do you bless someone who has cursed you?

_____

_____

_____

How do you bless those who have abused you?

_____

_____

_____

Why should you give people you think to be enemies space and not rush them to accept you?

_____

_____

_____

Please help me stop being careless with the use of the word enemy. I do not want to judge people too harshly lest I be judged harshly myself. Help me remember that often the people who irritate or hurt me are just being human. I will pray for them in love, I will extend grace and the benefit of the doubt to them. I ask you to bless those who probably are my real enemies. Heal their hearts and meet their needs. Cause them to walk in favor and good will. I will forgive them and I ask you to forgive them, too. Thank you, Jesus, for helping me to learn how to recognize the truth. Amen.

APPLES of GOLD
in BASKETS
of SILVER
Proverbs 25:11

Golden Apple Eight

The Ripple Effect Of Blessing

*"And his master saw that the LORD was with him and that the LORD made
all he did to prosper in his hand. So Joseph found favor in his sight . . . So it
was, from the time that he had made him overseer of his house and all that
he had, that the LORD blessed the Egyptian's house for Joseph's sake;
and the blessing of the LORD was on all that he
had in the house and in the field."*

(Genesis 39:3-5, *NKJV*)

Potipher the Egyptian was not a man of God, yet non-believers know when someone walks closely with the Lord. They also know when a great show of spirituality is nothing but pretense. Many unsaved people are drawn to the display of God's goodness in those He blesses, and they extend favor to them as well.

I recently read a true story about a church youth group that had a bus breakdown in the Midwest. Upon checking with the local garage, they learned it was going to be several days before a new part would arrive. The youth leader went to a local church and asked if the youth group could sleep in the church building. He was turned down. He then went to a local motel and was trying to make arrangements that would take all of their money.

An unsaved yet sympathetic desk clerk related the situation to an unsaved woman who had a large ranch. She invited the entire youth group to stay at her ranch until their bus was fixed. The young people were fed marvelously, taught how to ride horses, and shown great hospitality all around. You can be sure that this woman received an overflow of blessing from God's hand upon those young people.

Lord, don't ever let me refuse to give hospitality to those you send to my door. I will walk carefully with you, listening to you, so people never have to wonder Who I believe and love. Amen.

126

Tasting The Truth

How do you think unbelievers recognize when someone walks closely with God?

_____

_____

_____

How do you think unbelievers recognize when someone is only pretending to be very spiritual?

_____

_____

_____

Why do you think pastors of a church would turn down a request to let a youth group sleep in their church? Do you think God could have been involved in this pastor's refusal? Why?

_____

_____

_____

_____

How do you think the "ripple effect" of blessing was going to work in this story?

_____

_____

_____

_____

I want to be able to share what I have with those who need help. Lord, help me get over my concern that the blessings you have given me might be abused by others. Help me to learn how to share and trust you with the details. If you blessed me once with nice things, you can bless me again. Or if I just need to lighten up a little, then teach me that, too. Amen.

Golden Apple Nine

Blessing Is Never Double-minded

"With their mouths they bless, but in their hearts they curse."

(Psalm 62:4, *NIV*)

James tells us in his Epistle in the Bible that anyone who is double-minded is unstable in all his way (James 1:8). One who is unstable is unable to plant his feet and stand on solid ground—always shifting positions. Regardless of how strong you might try to act, if you are double-minded it will always show in your conversations and your actions.

You are deceived as well as double-minded when you think that your words will not expose a heart that inwardly curses others. When the inward condition of your heart (soul) is contemptuous of another person, you don't have to say a word to cause your contempt to be revealed. An unanswered question, a shifting of the eyes, or a change of subject will convey the presence of such feelings.

Begin today to let God get to the source of ill feelings you have towards others. Only God can permanently uproot those feelings by healing the actual source of them. For Him to do this, He needs you to take down the fences and barricades around your inner garden where these thorns and thistles are entrenched. Begin to pray for the person you struggle with that he would be blessed, encouraged, and strengthened by God. Ask God to have others give him favor and prosper him. It is impossible to remain angry with someone you are praying love-prayers for. Then your mouth will be able to speak words of kindness, love, and life regarding him.

In Jesus' name, I loose and tear down all walls and barricades protecting ill feelings within my soul. Forgive me for them and help me to cast them out and replace them with love and grace and mercy towards those I have been angry with. Amen.

Tasting The Truth

What does it mean to be double-minded? Give an example of a double-minded man.

_____

_____

Do you think you can fool people about how you feel about another person? Do you think other people can fool you about how they feel about you?

_____

_____

_____

_____

Why is it the best plan to concentrate of getting God into the source of your problems instead of concentrating on the other person's problems?

_____

_____

_____

What do you have to do to cooperate with God?

_____

_____

Why do you think it is almost impossible to remain angry with someone you are praying love-prayers for?

_____

APPLES of GOLD
in BASKETS
of SILVER
Proverbs 25:11

I do not want to ever be double-minded. If I have bad feelings in my heart towards someone, then I will run to you and seek your help to fix me. I want to be able to plant my feet and hold my position. I want to be known as straightforward and truthful. Help me to always be honest with others. Amen.

Golden Apple Ten

Blessing God

"O God, You are my God; early will I seek You; My soul thirsts for You; my flesh longs for You in a dry and thirsty land where there is no water. So I have looked for You in the sanctuary, to see Your power and Your glory. Because Your lovingkindness is better than life, my lips shall praise You. Thus I will bless You while I live; I will lift up my hands in Your name."

(Psalm 63:1-4, *NKJV*)

You bless God by praise and thanksgiving as David did in 1 Chronicles 29:10-13, *"Blessed be thou, LORD God of Israel our father, for ever and ever. Thine, O LORD, is the greatness, and the power, and the glory, and the victory, and the majesty: for all that is in the heaven and in the earth is thine; thine is the kingdom, O LORD, and thou art exalted as head above all. Both riches and honour come of thee, and thou reignest over all; and in thine hand is power and might; and in thine hand it is to make great, and to give strength unto all. Now therefore, our God, we thank thee, and praise thy glorious name"* (*KJV*).

When blessing is directed to God, if possible it should be shared to inspire others to call out blessings to Him, too. *"Oh, bless our God, you peoples! And make the voice of His praise to be heard, who keeps our soul among the living, and does not allow our feet to be moved"* (Psalm 66:8-9 *NKJV*). Sing out a blessing to the Lord and encourage others to sing with you. *"Oh, sing to the LORD a new song! Sing to the LORD, all the earth. Sing to the LORD, bless His name; proclaim the good news of His salvation from day to day"* (Psalm 96:1-2, *NKJV*). Let the Holy Spirit melt your heart to love God and bless Him.

How I long to bless you, Father God, ruler of all the earth and Savior to me. You deserve all honor and glory from your people, and I will speak of you before all who will listen. Amen.

Tasting The Truth

In what book of the Bible are great praise and thanksgiving examples found?

_____

_____

_____

Find three other Scriptures that praise and give thanksgiving to God that you could use to bless Him. Write them here.

_____

_____

_____

_____

_____

When you direct blessing to God, what else should you do to multiply the effect?

_____

_____

What is another form of blessing God?

_____

_____

_____

Thank God here for blessing you by allowing you to be His messenger proclaiming the good news of His salvation.

_____

_____

I will praise you and thank you, I will make my voice heard so that others can bless you, too. Thank you for promising to see that my feet will not be moved. I sing a new song to you because of the love I have for you. I will proclaim your good news because everyone needs to know that you are a wonderful God. Teach me how to cause others to join me as I do this. Amen.

Silver Basket

7

CONVINCED BUT NOT CHANGED

Golden Apple One

Do Words Or Actions Speak Louder?

"If you confess with your mouth, 'Jesus is Lord,' and believe in your heart that God raised Him from the dead, you will be saved."

(Romans 10:9-10, *NIV*)

*T*he Apostle Paul told these Roman Christians that we are saved by speaking words of faith with our mouths. If you believe these words as you say them, there appears to be no other conditions or tasks you must fulfill to receive salvation.

Now consider the sons whose father asked them to work in his vineyard (Matthew 21:28-32). The first son said no, but then changed his mind and did as his father has asked. The second son said yes, but then didn't do anything. Jesus likened ignorant sinners to the son who first said no, and who then changed their minds and did what the Father asked. Then Jesus likened the second son to the priests and elders of the temple standing there questioning Him, for they had seemingly said yes to God yet they were not doing what He wanted.

Paul seemed to say words alone are enough. Jesus seemed to say that actions are more important than words. In Romans, Paul was actually talking about words of faith being the <u>means of obtaining salvation</u>. Jesus was speaking about actions being the <u>evidence of salvation</u>. There is only one way to become saved—by faith. But once you are saved, there should be an outward evidence of your state of salvation in your actions and deeds. These are not works to prove you are saved, they come out of enjoying and appreciating being saved.

My faith has brought me your salvation by the confession of my mouth. Now help me, Jesus, to remember to loose everything out of my soul that would prevent a natural outpouring of the visible evidence that I am indeed saved. Amen.

Tasting The Truth

Do you believe that your confession of faith in Jesus Christ as your Savior was enough to become saved? Why?

_____

_____

_____

Find and write here one other seeming contradiction of Scripture that you have not understood. Ask the Father to show you the truth of it and then record His answer.

_____

_____

_____

Do you understand the difference between not doing works to obtain favor with God, but your works being the evidence of your love for Jesus? Explain your answer here.

_____

_____

_____

_____

Pray and ask God to reveal whether or not you have that evidence, or if you are doing works to obtain His favor. Write His answer here.

_____

_____

_____

APPLES of GOLD
in BASKETS
of SILVER
Proverbs 25:11

I have confessed Jesus Christ as my Lord and Savior by the words of my mouth. I believed them, and He saved me. Thank you, Father, for such a plan of salvation. I know that I do not have to do works to deserve my salvation, but I am pleased that my good works are simply the evidence of my salvation bubbling out of me. Thank you, Father. Amen.

Golden Apple Two

What Measure Is In You?

"But to each one of us grace was given according to the measure of Christ's gift . . . For I say, through the grace given to me, to everyone who is among you, not to think of himself more highly than he ought to think, but to think soberly, as God has dealt to each one a measure of faith."

(Ephesians 4:7; Romans 12:3, *NKJV*)

The word "measure" means just a portion or a partial amount. This implies that there is more. The whole measure that we must keep pressing into God for is the *"measure of the stature of the fullness of Christ"* (Ephesians 4:13, *NKJV*). Don't ever be a Christian who made it to the foot of the cross and camped.

How do you find the fullness of that measure of Christ? Consider how God has designed you. Have you tried to control your own design? If you are still trying to control your life and your destiny, then you do not trust Jesus to use your life in a manner that will fulfill and bless you. The fullness of Christ will give you peace about trusting God's plans as He did.

Your character must be as strong as or stronger than the gifts God gives you. Be very consistent with the Word of God to check yourself. *"This Book of the Law shall not depart from your mouth, but you shall meditate in it day and night, that you may observe to do according to all that is written in it. For then you will make your way prosperous, and then you will have good success"* Joshua 1:8, *NKJV*). Let the Word of God work out any wrong motives you might have for using your gifts. It can cut between soul and spirit.

Dear Father, I don't want to be a Christian who camped at the cross and never moved in any direction. I want to have the fullness of Christ within me so I can go forth and share. I want to spread the Good News everywhere. Amen.

Tasting The Truth

What does the word measure mean? What does it imply?

_____

_____

_____

Explain your understanding of the sentence: Don't ever be a Christian who made it to the foot of the cross and camped.

_____

_____

_____

_____

How do you think God has made you and why are you unique from others? Do you think you have tried to change or control His original design for you?

_____

_____

_____

If you do try to control your life and destiny, what does that mean?

_____

_____

Write here your understanding of this sentence: Your character must be as strong or stronger than the gifts God has given you.

_____

_____

Please show me more clearly what measure I have been given of grace and faith. Sometimes I am not sure what I do have, but you have said that you would answer my questions. If I have tried to control how you designed me because of fear of man, forgive me, Father. I want a strong character and I want a strong sense of my purpose and what you want. I want to be all you created me to be. Amen.

Golden Apple Three

Self-Righteous Anger Is Never Holy Anger

"Be angry, and yet do not sin; do not let the sun go down on your anger, and do not give the devil an opportunity."

(Ephesians 4:26-27, *NAS*)

Once we have locked defenses of logic, rationalizations, and justifications into place, thereby creating a stronghold, we stop growing. This keeps us from becoming who God says we can be: peacemakers and overcomers who are filled with power, healing, and grace. How do you avoid these defenses?

Unchecked anger and pain always initiate stronghold-building. Be very aware whenever anyone offends, lies to, or tricks you so that you do not react to the offense with indignation and anger. You give the devil a foothold and opportunity in your life whenever you do (Ephesians 4:27, *Amplified*). When you choose to justify your anger over an offense (no matter how big in your eyes), it becomes big trouble for you <u>as soon as the sun goes down that night</u> (see Ephesians 4:26). Anger is to be dealt with before the sun goes down, giving a maximum twenty-three hours, fifty-nine minutes, and fifty-nine seconds time frame to let it go (depending on when you got mad).

Be careful not to try excusing your anger and offenses by calling your feelings a holy anger. Holy anger, such as Jesus exhibited in the temple with the money changers, is pretty rare. Our anger is about 99 percent self-righteousness every time. God gave us the powerful emotion of anger because it helps us be bold and courageous when we need to. Pray for self-control that you will use your anger well.

I need your help to know how to control my anger, Lord. I do not want to turn it on other people for personal gain or revenge. I bind my soul to your will and I loose all old patterns of emotional thinking and reactions. I will not be bound by anger. Amen.

Tasting The Truth

How do we create strongholds?

_____

_____

What happens when we do build strongholds?

_____

_____

What does this keep from us?

_____

_____

If someone offends or lies to you, what should you be very aware of?

_____

_____

How do you avoid building stronghold defenses to justify your anger?

_____

_____

_____

What do strongholds give the devil?

_____

_____

Why did God give us this easily out-of-control emotion, anger?

_____

_____

APPLES of GOLD
in BASKETS
of SILVER
Proverbs 25:11

Lord, I do not want my anger to be out of control. You gave me this emotion, so please teach me to use it only when necessary. Help me to never try to excuse my anger, but only to ask forgiveness if I hurt anyone with it. Amen.

Golden Apple Four

Will You Let God Be God In Your Life?

"'For My thoughts are not your thoughts, nor are your ways My ways,' says the LORD. 'For as the heavens are higher than the earth, so are My ways higher than your ways, and My thoughts than your thoughts.'"

(Isaiah 55:8-9, *NKJV*)

God is in control of your destiny and your daily life. There is no thing and no one in the world who can alter His purposes for your life except your own unsurrendered soul. While I'm not sure we can alter His ultimate plans, I do know that we can alter His time frame when we are in disobedience. The length of the journey, not the final destination, always keeps coming back to the choices you make.

If you are desperately, frantically waiting on God for an answer, you must first stop feeling desperate and frantic—that is an old cycle of your unsurrendered soul that will get you nowhere. God is never desperate or frantic over the resolution of any situation. He is actually far more interested in fulfilling His eternal purposes for your life than He is in reacting to your temporal fit of panic. Your Father will never allow any hard thing to happen to you without an underlying purpose for good.

God is always looking at the long-term perspective, so try to relax. While you're waiting for your answer, if you need something to occupy your time, concentrate on what God is doing in the lives of those around you. You may realize that He wants to display something so unbelievable through your situation that you'll hate yourself for the rest of your earthly life if you mess it up or miss out on it!

I hadn't thought of looking around to see who else is in close proximity to what I'm going through. It would be exciting to know that this is for someone else's good, God. Amen.

Tasting The Truth

Only one person can alter God's purposes for your life, who is that?

_____

How do we alter His time frame for our destiny purposes?

_____

_____

Feeling frantic and desperate is a symptom of what?

_____

_____

Your Father will never allow anything hard to happen to you without what?

_____

God always looks at everything from what perspective?

_____

If time is moving slow for you, what should you try to concentrate upon?

_____

_____

God is far more interested in fulfilling His eternal purposes in your life than He is in what?

_____

The length of the journey, not the final destination, always comes back to your what?

_____

_____

APPLES of GOLD
in BASKETS
of SILVER
Proverbs 25:11

Lord, thank you for controlling my destiny and my daily life, at least controlling it as much as you can with me getting in your way all the time. I want to become calm and relaxed about what you are doing in my life, and cooperate. Amen.

Golden Apple Five

Have You Really Gotten Out Of The Driver's Seat?

"Let me put this question to you: How did your new life begin? Was it by working your heads off to please God? Or was it by responding to God's Message to you? Are you going to continue this craziness? For only crazy people would think they could complete by their own efforts what was begun by God."

(Galatians 3:2-3, *The Message*)

Many Christians don't even think about surrendering to Jesus Christ until they have exhausted their own resources—mental, emotional, and financial. At that point they may be losers by the world's standards, but when they do surrender they have just caught the diamond ring by heaven's standard

The soul in itself profits us nothing except as a vehicle of expression for our regenerated spirits. Amazingly, the human soul wants to drive even though it is just a vehicle designed to <u>transport something more important than itself</u>. Our souls have attempted to usurp the roles of the vehicle owner, the driver, the mechanic, and even the body shop. Our souls also have attempted to mentally, emotionally, and willfully finesse or ram (whatever seems appropriate to them) their way through all the traffic jams of our lives. This brings confusion, stress, and anxiety to our entire makeup, including our body.

A lot of personal stress is relieved when we kick our souls out of the driver's seat and let our Lord and Master drive. He is so good at it, it is ridiculous to fight Him for the wheel! Please consider letting Him take over so you can rest in Him and be refreshed for opportunities coming.

Wow, what a concept, God—let you worry about driving and directing my life. I love it. You are the vehicle owner, the driver, the mechanic, and the body shop. I'm yours. Amen.

Tasting The Truth

Many Christians don't even think about surrendering to Jesus Christ until what point?

_____

_____

_____

The soul in itself profits no one except as a what?

_____

_____

Then the soul wants to do what?

_____

_____

This causes what to happen?

_____

_____

How can we relieve a lot of our personal stress?

_____

_____

Write God a short thank you note right here for wanting to take over all of the stress and responsibility of your life so that you can just love and obey.

_____

_____

_____

APPLES of GOLD in BASKETS of SILVER Proverbs 25:11

I need to always remember that Jesus never ran around worrying about where things were and why people didn't like Him. I'm sorry that I get so self-focused sometimes, please forgive me. Help me to focus outside of myself. Help me to ride in the back of the vehicle and enjoy being driven around. I love you, Lord, and I appreciate all that you do for me. Amen.

Golden Apple Six

Who Controls Your Thoughts?

"Since, then, you have been raised with Christ, set your hearts on things above, where Christ is seated at the right hand of God. Set your minds on things above, not on earthly things."

(Colossians 3:1-2, *NIV*)

When your soul is left to its own devices, it will usually try to find ways to intellectualize making self-centered choices while over analyzing its feelings about everything. If your soul is feeling fearful or doubtful, it tends to get carried away with those emotions. For years we've been told that since we have all authority in Jesus Christ, we just need to take authority over our fears and doubts. This is not a practical suggestion. Think about where fear and doubt reside. In your soul. What part of you "takes authority" over anything? Your soul.

Have you ever tried to tell your mind it was not afraid when it was? Have you ever tried to tell your emotions they were not upset when they were? Have you ever tried to reverse your will when it was in full "charge" mode? All three parts of an unsurrendered soul are determined to think, feel, and do whatever and however they want. Your soul will not take "authority" over any part of itself that it doesn't want to.

The only real victory I've ever had with my soul when it is in its "stubborn mode" has been to bind it to God's will and let Him work on it. That seems like not taking responsibility for my own soul, but it is a very real and practical way to get a spiritual tune up on your thoughts, feelings, and self-will. God is always pleased to be asked to do it.

I need that spiritual tune up, Lord. I bind my soul to your will and I loose all of its controlling thought patterns. I've tried to take authority over it and I've tried to analyze it. Now I need you to work on it. I give you permission. Amen.

144

Tasting The Truth

Why can't you let your soul try to fix things on its own?

_____

_____

_____

Even if you think "taking authority" over your feelings has worked for you, there will come a day when it all comes down. Why is it impractical to try to control your soul this way?

_____

_____

_____

What is one sure way to deal with a stubborn soul?

_____

_____

_____

Is this not being accountable or taking responsibility for your own actions?

_____

_____

What does the term "spiritual tune up" mean to you?

_____

_____

_____

APPLES of GOLD in BASKETS of SILVER Proverbs 25:11

I want to set my heart on things above and let you fine tune things down here below. I've tried "taking authority" over myself and it has not worked. So I'm giving you the reins. Please give me a spiritual tune up and let me know if I am not taking care of the self-maintenance of my soul. I will cooperate with you however you say. Amen.

Golden Apple Seven

Fresh Attitudes

"Be constantly renewed in the spirit of your mind—having a fresh mental and spiritual attitude; and put on the new nature (the regenerate self) created in God's image."

(Ephesians 4:23-24, *Amplified*)

Sometimes our souls like to run artificial attitudes that are appealing to others. These artificial attitudes must be maintained by constant vigilance of the soul. A genuine fresh mental and spiritual attitude is not a role; it is a reality that requires no rehearsing or soulish maintenance. It is a state of being in Him. God let Paul be put in prison where he would write Epistles that would impact time and eternity. What if Paul had gone to prison in a fit of righteous indignation, with bad attitudes flying? What if he had tried to call God's bluff?

Probably wondering why it was happening, Paul nevertheless adjusted his attitude to obedience and waited for God's full plans to be revealed. When you feel that you have prayed, obeyed, and stayed as long as you can, the best course of action is still to hold steady and let God be God. Your spirit believes God knows what He's doing, but your unsurrendered soul does not. It wants to bolt and run in any direction it can.

Double-minded believers have the carnal mind of their souls in conflict with the mind of Christ in their spirits. These believers will anxiously fret over the consequences of letting God take over or not letting God take over. A spiritually free believer has the mind of Christ in him with Christ's peace and input empowering his attitudes and beliefs. This person calmly waits for God's signal light to turn green.

I want to slow down and patiently wait for your green lights, Lord. I'm tired of my soul hot rodding through life. I want an attitude adjustment so that I can be at peace like Paul. Amen.

Tasting The Truth

What is the difference between your soul's artificial attitudes and a genuine spiritual attitude?

_____

_____

_____

What do you think Paul might have been wondering when he ended up in prison instead of out preaching? What would you have wondered?

_____

_____

_____

When you feel you have prayed, obeyed, and stayed as long as you can, what should you do then?

_____

_____

_____

Double-minded believers have what conflict going on in their souls?

_____

_____

Write a prayer here committing yourself to waiting on God, listening for His direction and waiting for His signal.

_____

_____

I so want to be a spiritually free believer, I don't want to be reacting and fretting over whether or not to let you run my life. Please help me as I loose that kind of attitude from my mind. I need your peace and input empowering my attitudes. Amen.

Golden Apple Eight

You Can Be Free, But Do You Want To Be?

"Forgetting what is behind and straining toward what is ahead, I press on toward the goal to win the prize for which God has called me heavenward in Christ Jesus."

(Philippians 3:13-14, *NIV*)

I always wanted to know how to forget what was in my past. Once I even asked God for holy amnesia. He said no. God does not heal us by altering facts and wiping out what has happened, because He is a God of truth. Instead He proves that His love, grace, and mercy are so powerful that He can neutralize pain, nullify shame, and replace ashes with beauty and freedom.

The word forgetting (as used above) means to stop caring for something and to begin neglecting it. In other words, stop taking care of those memories, stop fertilizing them and reinforcing them by constantly rerunning them in both your mind and to those who will listen.

When you cling to every bad memory, painful thought, and offense you have ever experienced, peace, healing, and victory will not come to you. You must give the Holy Spirit access into your soul to heal your hurts, meet your needs, and make you whole. Otherwise, whatever bitterness and unforgiveness you're packing around, whatever neediness is driving you, whatever confusion and pain you feel will ooze out of you and touch everything and everyone you get near. No matter how hard you try to contain your pain, it will always leak out.

Jesus, I want to stop caring for my pain, and I want to start neglecting it so that there is nothing left to fertilize or rerun. I don't know how I got into the cycle of reinforcing my bad memories, but right now I loose all of my thought patterns that have caused me to do that. I now declare my memories to be in your control. Amen.

Tasting The Truth

God does not heal us by altering facts and wiping out what happened because:

_____

_____

Instead, He just proves what?

_____

_____

What is the original Greek meaning for the word "forgetting" as Paul used it when speaking to the Philippians?

_____

_____

What might be another reason for God not choosing to wipe bad memories out of your mind?

_____

_____

_____

How do you think you can give the Holy Spirit access into your soul?

_____

_____

_____

What can you end up doing to others if you don't let Him heal you?

_____

_____

Lord, I'm feeling better and I think I'm learning to cooperate with you. Thank you for working so patiently with me. Bless you, Lord, and I praise your holy name. I like what I'm feeling and I'm happier than I've ever been. Thank you. Amen.

Golden Apple Nine

Nurture Your Conscience

"To the pure, all things are pure, but to those who are corrupted and do not believe, nothing is pure. In fact, both their minds and consciences are corrupted."

(Titus 1:15, *NIV*)

*T*hayer's *Greek-English Lexicon* explains our consciences as that part of us that has "joint knowledge" with the Holy Spirit. *Vine's Dictionary* says that the conscience is the faculty by which we apprehend the will of God. *Nelson's Bible Dictionary* says that the conscience is our inner awareness of when we are conforming to or departing from the will of God.

The conscience is a part of the human soul developed by observing other examples of right consciences, having right teaching, and by the washing of the Word. The human soul will try to compensate for a guilty conscience, but in Hebrews 9:9, Paul said that gifts and sacrifices offered for sin were not able to clear the conscience of the worshiper. The conscience can only be cleansed by repenting and receiving the washing of the blood of Christ as read in Hebrews 9:14. Ignoring the warning of a good conscience can produce a seared conscience—scarred and deadened—which is a fearful thing. Such a deadened conscience must exist in the mind of one who will kill, rape, and torture other human beings without a second thought.

Paul told Timothy to hold onto his good conscience, because without it some had shipwrecked their faith. Paul also said he tended his own conscience. Search out examples of other's good conscience decisions and read of them in the Word.

Lord Jesus, please forgive me for the sins and wrongs I have committed that have stained my conscience. I ask you to cleanse my conscience as I study the Word of the Father to nurture and strengthen its ability to choose right. Amen.

Tasting The Truth

List the different explanations of the conscience.

_____

_____

_____

God gave us our consciences, but how do we develop them?

_____

_____

_____

What do you think can cause someone to have a weak conscience?

_____

_____

_____

How can you cleanse your conscience from the stain of sin?

_____

_____

How do you get a seared conscience?

_____

_____

Paul said he tended his conscience. What do you think that means?

_____

_____

Lord, I do not ever want my conscience to be stained or seared. I want it to always remain tender towards your warnings and dealings. Jesus, I'm asking you to wash my conscience now, and I bind my mind to yours so I can hear you speak to me. Amen.

Golden Apple Ten

A Cleansed Conscience

"The blood of goats and bulls and the ashes of a heifer sprinkled on those who are ceremonially unclean sanctify them so that they are outwardly clean. How much more, then, will the blood of Christ, who through the eternal Spirit offered himself unblemished to God, cleanse our consciences."

(Hebrews 9:13-14, *NIV*)

If your conscience is troubled, there are no sacrifices you can make, no good deeds, no willing yourself to a new behavior that can purge your sense of guilt. You can try to deny the guilt and to shove it away which is the beginning of moving towards searing your conscience. Well-intentioned acts of good deeds and trying to act out new behaviors are not wrong in themselves, but they can never wash away guilt or cleanse your conscience from the stain of sin.

The purifying of our consciences comes only by the washing of the blood of Jesus. Matthew Henry says "Christ's blood is sufficient to enable us to serve the living God, not only by purging away that guilt which separates between God and sinners, but by sanctifying and renewing the soul through the gracious influences of the Holy Spirit."

Matthew Henry also says meddling with sin fixes defilement in the soul, and only the blood of Jesus can purge it out.

Jesus, please cleanse my conscience and make it fresh and new. I do not want any hardening of my conscience, any searing or cauterizing that would make it scarred and insensitive. Forgive me for having dulled my senses by exposure to things that would have shocked me ten years ago. Lord, please don't ever let me become complacent about the world's doings in these days. I love you and I thank you. Amen.

Tasting The Truth

What do we often try to do when our consciences are troubled?

_____

_____

_____

What is the only way to purify our consciences? Write a short prayer here repenting and asking Jesus to wash your conscience of any impurity that is in it.

_____

_____

_____

What sanctifies and renews the soul?

_____

_____

What does Matthew Henry say about defilement in the soul? What do you think this means?

_____

_____

_____

Thank Jesus here for shedding His blood to cleanse you.

_____

_____

APPLES of GOLD
in BASKETS
of SILVER
Proverbs 25:11

The blood of Jesus is my lifeline, my answer to everything I need, and my heart's nourishment. Please never let me take it for granted. I need a thorough cleansing of my conscience not only from deliberate sin, but from just walking in the world today with all of its defilement. Make me clean, Lord, so I can continue to walk out into the world and set captives free. Amen.

Silver Basket

FRUIT OF THE SPIRIT

Golden Apple One

Nine Gorgeous Fruit

"The fruit of the Spirit is love, joy, peace, longsuffering, kindness, goodness, faithfulness, gentleness, self-control. Against such there is no law."

Galatians 5:22-23, (*NKJV*)

There is an ongoing struggle between the unsurrendered soul and the born-again spirit in every one of us. Our soul strives against our born-again spirits while energetically resisting every work of the Holy Spirit. Our renewed spirits strive against and oppose the wills of our unsurrendered souls, wrestling with the residue of sin and carnality in them.

Because the condition and state of your soul spills over into every area of your life, every moment you are in the presence of other people your conversation and behaviors are either drawing them towards or pushing them away from wanting what you have in Christ. As a believer, everything you say or do impacts someone.

The fruit of the Spirit are the sweet products of Christ's goodness that are resident within the Incorruptible Seed of Life He implanted within our born-again spirits when we accepted Him as our Savior. The proof of the presence of Jesus being welcome within a life is the fruit of the Spirit. Does your life prove He has been made welcome within you?

The fruit of the Spirit make the Christian a most delightful and agreeable person to be around. The invisible power of the Holy Spirit in those who are in Christ reproduce fruitful attributes which suggest a oneness with the character of the Lord.

To have any attribute which suggests I might be like my Father is a precious thing to me. I want to learn how to resist every attribute of my soul that would oppose this fruit in me. Amen.

Tasting The Truth

Write out the list of the fruit of the Spirit.

_____

_____

_____

Describe your understanding of the struggle that goes on between the unsurrendered soul and the born-again spirit within you.

_____

_____

_____

How do you impact other people every time you come into any form of contact with them?

_____

_____

What are the fruit of the Spirit actually products of?

_____

_____

_____

What is the proof of the presence of Jesus Christ within you?

_____

_____

_____

APPLES of GOLD
in BASKETS
of SILVER
Proverbs 25:11

I so want to have all of the fruit of the Spirit flowing out of me every day, Lord. I will loose all wrong patterns of thinking and all wrong attitudes in my soul that would resist the Holy Spirit and try to block His effects in my life. I want others to know that you are welcome and present within me. Amen.

Golden Apple Two

The Fruit Of Love

"A new command I give you: Love one another. As I have loved you, so you must love one another. By this all men will know that you are my disciples, if you love one another."

(John 13:34-35, *NIV*)

We are known as being disciples of Christ if we love one another. We are not identified because of our charities, our good works, or our fine preaching. We are not recognized as Christians because we help others; Muslims, atheists, and New Age people all helped when September 11, 2001, happened. We will be known as His as we show love one for another.

Love is the first of the nine spiritual fruit of His Spirit. Love (listed in 1 Corinthians 13:4-7) is patient, is kind, is not jealous, never brags, is not arrogant, does not act rude, is not self-seeking, is not easily angered, keeps no record of wrongs, rejoices in righteousness, rejoices in truth, always protects others, always trusts, always hopes, and endures all things. If these attributes are not yours in some measure, you have a clogged-up soul and you need the plunger of the Word!

The Words says: *"If someone says, 'I love God, and <u>hates</u> his brother, he is a liar; for he who does not love his brother whom he has seen, how can he love God whom he has not seen?'"* (1 John 4:20-21, *NKJV*). *Hate* as used here means: to love less, to postpone esteem, to slight, to disregard, and to be indifferent towards. I realized I said I loved one particularly difficult person, but I did not esteem him and was indifferent to him. That sent me back on my knees!

Jesus, if I am to be like you, then I must begin to act like you. I bind myself to the Father's will and to your mind. I loose all of my preconceived ideas about whether or not I love other people when the list above seems to say I really don't. Amen.

Tasting The Truth

How are we going to be known to be His disciples?

_____

_____

Describe how we try to show we are Christians by our good works and helping others.

_____

_____

Can you remember when one word, one look, or one remark caused you to suddenly realize that someone's seemingly loving help and deeds were not motivated by love? How did it make you feel?

_____

_____

_____

List five attributes of love that most strike you as what you want to be known for.

_____

_____

_____

List people you say you love, but you now realize that you do not esteem them and you are indifferent to them. Commit that you will begin to pray about your attitudes towards them.

_____

_____

I will loose all wrong patterns of thinking and all wrong attitudes in my soul that would contend with the love fruit of the Spirit within me to try to block its effects. I want others to know that I am definitely one of your disciples. Amen.

Golden Apple Three

The Fruit Of Joy

*"For the kingdom of God is not a matter of eating and drinking, but of
righteousness, peace and joy in the Holy Spirit, because anyone
who serves Christ in this way is pleasing to
God and approved by men"*

(Romans 14:17-18, *NIV*)

What is the first thing others say when they are trying to describe you?
That's a sobering thought, isn't it? I don't think that they say that I have a lot of
joy. They might say I'm a good teacher or I'm funny or something else, but I've
never heard anyone say they thought I was full of joy. I want to have joy that
overflows and splashes onto other people.

Jesus said to His followers, *"If ye keep my commandments, ye shall abide in my
love; even as I have kept my Father's commandments, and abide in his love.
These things have I spoken unto you, that my joy might remain in you, and that
your joy might be full"* (John 15:10-11, *KJV*). Our first clue to finding joy is in
obedience.

Several New Testament writers speak of their joy as coming from seeing
success, growth, and joy in others. Paul said to the Roman Christians, *"Everyone
has heard about your obedience, so I am full of joy over you."* He said to the
Philippians Christians, *"Make my joy complete by being like-minded, having the
same love, being one in spirit and purpose."* John said, *"I have no greater joy
than to hear that my children walk in truth."* One common use of the word joy
in the Old Testament is *simchah*, meaning to be bright and to shine. Joy exudes
bright and shiny feelings.

*Lord, I bind myself to you and I loose all wrong patterns of thinking that would
block your joy within me. I want to have bright and shiny feelings to share with
others. Amen.*

Tasting The Truth

What does the above verse say the Kingdom of God contains?

_____

_____

_____

How do you think other people describe you?

_____

_____

_____

_____

What is a good clue to finding joy?

_____

_____

What times have you had when you have felt great joy because you saw someone else succeed or show real growth?

_____

_____

_____

What does the Hebrew word *simchah* mean?

_____

_____

_____

I need a fresh infusion of your joy, Lord. I think I have had some wrong ideas about obeying you. I want to obey you with joy while having my joy increased. I want to feel great joy over the successes of others. I want shiny and bright joy to spill out of me so that is the first thing people think of about me. I want to be a translucent vessel that shows forth your joy. I just want to fill up with joy and then turn around and splash it out on others. Thank you, Lord. Amen.

Golden Apple Four

The Fruit of Peace

"Peace I leave with you, my peace I give unto you: not as the world giveth, give I unto you. Let not your heart be troubled, neither let it be afraid."

(John 14:27, *KJV*)

How can we embrace the occasionally elusive fruit of the Spirit called peace? The Word gives us several clues. *"Great peace have they who love your law, and nothing can make them stumble"* (Psalms 119:165, *NIV*). Peace comes from loving His Word and His commandments. *"You will keep him in perfect peace, whose mind is stayed on You, because he trusts in You"* (Isaiah 26:3, *NKJV*). Stayed in this verse means upheld, firm, unchanging. When we are unchanging about focusing our mind on Him, He upholds us and gives us peace.

James said, *"The wisdom that is from above is first pure, then peaceable, gentle, willing to yield, full of mercy and good fruits, without partiality and without hypocrisy. Now the fruit of righteousness is sown in peace by those who make peace"* (James 3:17-18, *NKJV*).

The Israelites were even told to pray for the peace of the city where they were being held captive. *"Seek the peace of the city where I have caused you to be carried away captive, and pray to the LORD for it; for in its peace you will have peace"* (Jeremiah 29:7, *NKJV*). Are you seeking to spread peace into other peoples' troubles and trials, or are you too busy wrestling alligators in your own swamp?

Lord, I want to be a peacemaker and a peacekeeper. I bind my mind to the mind of Christ and I loose all stressful, negative, and fearful thoughts from my own mind. Show me how to receive peace and speak peace into others. I want to seek the peace of my city. Thank you for the peace you give. Amen.

Tasting The Truth

Where does peace come from?

_____

_____

_____

What can we do to cooperate with receiving peace?

_____

_____

_____

_____

What does it mean that our mind is stayed on Him?

_____

_____

_____

Write a short prayer here in which you pray for the peace of your city.

_____

_____

_____

_____

Can you think of some "alligators" you need to loose to create room within yourself to receive His peace?

_____

_____

I will fix my thoughts and my focus upon your Word because it will keep me sure-footed and in peace. I will keep my thoughts and my focus on you, Lord, because when my mind is on you, you will keep me in peace. I love to think about you and who you are. I cannot think exclusively of you and worry at the same time! Hallelujah! Amen.

Golden Apple Five

The Fruit of Longsuffering

"I, therefore, the prisoner of the Lord, beseech you to walk worthy of the calling with which you were called, with all lowliness and gentleness, with longsuffering, bearing with one another in love, endeavoring to keep the unity of the Spirit in the bond of peace."

(Ephesians 4:1-3, *NKJV*)

Longsuffering is a fruit of the Spirit that is so clearly seen in the attributes of God himself—great and enduring patience, patience that goes on and on. I'm very grateful for that. To be humanly patient is one thing, but to be patient with great endurance is a truly divine fruit. Had God not been longsuffering towards me, I can only wonder where I would be now. We can all say thank you, Lord, to that!

Longsuffering means patience, endurance, constancy, steadfastness, and slowness in avenging wrongs. Longsuffering always bears with others' shortcomings, loving them while ever working at keeping the unity of the Spirit which is the bond of peace.

Paul told Timothy (1 Timothy 1:16, *NKJV*), *"For this reason I obtained mercy, that in me first Jesus Christ might show all longsuffering, as a pattern to those who are going to believe on Him for everlasting life."* The fruit of longsuffering needs to be drawn out of our spirits and into our souls so that our lives might be a visual pattern of Jesus Christ's great enduring patience to those who are going to believe on Him.

I do not always want to be patient, but I set my will to learn how to desire this fruit of the Spirit in all my dealings with others. Never let me forget how much patience you have had with me. Let me see others with your love and a willingness to wait for their growth in you. Amen.

Tasting The Truth

Why do we need longsuffering to bear with one another in love?

_____

_____

_____

Stop and think where you might be today if God had not been longsuffering towards you. Write Him a thank you note right here.

_____

_____

_____

_____

What does longsuffering mean?

_____

_____

_____

We are to endeavor to keep the unity of the Spirit in the bond of peace. What do you think that means?

_____

_____

_____

How are we to become patterns of Christ?

_____

_____

APPLES of GOLD
in BASKETS
of SILVER
Proverbs 25:11

I need to have all of the fruit of the Spirit coming out of me every day, Lord. I will loose all wrong patterns of thinking and all wrong attitudes in my soul that would contend with the fruit of the Spirit and try to block its effects. I want others to know that you are present within me. Amen.

Golden Apple Six

The Fruit of Kindness

"Therefore, as God's chosen people, holy and dearly loved, clothe yourselves with compassion, kindness, humility, gentleness and patience. Bear with each other and forgive whatever grievances you may have against one another. Forgive as the Lord forgave you. And over all these virtues put on love, which binds them all together in perfect unity."

(Colossians 3:12-14, *NIV*)

God himself is filled with kindness towards mankind. Titus 3:4-5 (*NIV*) tells us, *"But when the kindness and love of God our Savior appeared, he saved us, not because of righteous things we had done, but because of his mercy."* What a thrill to hope for the fruit of His Spirit to cause even a small part of that attribute in Him to become rooted and growing within us to bless others.

Kindness means moral goodness and integrity according the original Greek language. This infers that the spiritual fruit of kindness never has an ulterior motive, never has a hidden agenda, and is produced to benefit others.

When I was a year old in the Lord. I remember saying something very unkind to someone who made a very embarrassing mistake in the church office where I worked. Later that same day, I committed a far more embarrassing mistake. I was humiliated because the person I had been unkind to was standing right there. This person graciously pretended not to have seen what I had done and quickly attracted everyone's attention to something outside. That was undeserved kindness and grace that I will never forget.

Lord, show me how to be kind and gracious to everyone. I want to encourage others with your kindness. I want to always practice your Word which says to be kind to all. Amen.

Tasting The Truth

What do you think it means to clothe yourself with kindness?

_____

_____

_____

_____

How does it make you feel to know that God's Spirit wants to impart God's attribute of kindness through your spirit and your soul?

_____

_____

_____

What does the word kindness mean in the N.T. Greek language.

_____

_____

_____

What does this meaning infer?

_____

_____

_____

_____

Can you remember undeserved acts of kindness and grace that others have extended towards you? List them here and then pray and ask God to bless them (or their loved ones if they are in heaven) today.

_____

_____

APPLES of GOLD
in BASKETS
of SILVER
Proverbs 25:11

I have known much kindness from other people. Lord, I have so many to thank for showing me your love until I could actually know it was you all along. Help me to fulfill this debt of love to many, please. I am thrilled to be able to kind to others. Let my kindness cause other acts of kindness to grow. Amen.

Golden Apple Seven

The Fruit of Goodness

"For you were once darkness, but now you are light in the Lord.
Live as children of light (for the fruit of the light consists
in all goodness, righteousness and truth)
and find out what pleases the Lord."

(Ephesians 5:8-10, *NIV*)

Most of the references in the Bible regarding goodness are used to express the goodness (kindness, gentleness, patience) of God towards us. What another wonderful character trait that He is willing to give us by His Spirit. In life today, so many people act out of their feelings during a given situation. saying things like, *"I was going to be nice and do something good for you, but then you gave me that look I don't like. So I didn't."*

Such excuses are based upon situational ethics—moral principles and corresponding behaviors that change with every situation. When you don't believe in absolutes, you will act out of situational ethics. God's goodness in the Incorruptible Seed of Life in your spirit is an absolute.

We should always treat others with goodness, whether we like them or not. Goodness (original Hebrew) means to be pleasant, do well, do right, confer benefits, be fair, and make cheerful. This is not an aggressive fruit of the Spirit (perhaps none of them really are). Rather it seeks to grow in souls where there are no unkind, negative thoughts. *"Let us not become weary in doing good, for at the proper time we will reap a harvest if we do not give up"* (Galatians 6:9, *NIV*).

I want the fruit of goodness flowing steadily out of my soul into my spirit, Lord. I bind my will to yours so that my soul is obligated to your desires and your leading in my life. So many need to know your goodness and I thank you for every time that you have allowed me to demonstrate it to them. Amen.

Tasting The Truth

Goodness coexists with what else in the fruit of His light?

_____

_____

_____

How is the goodness of God described?

_____

_____

_____

How would you describe situational ethics? Give an example of situational ethics.

_____

_____

_____

_____

_____

_____

_____

Look up the word absolute in the dictionary and write its meaning here.

_____

_____

_____

What are the characteristics of goodness that are working their way out of you?

_____

_____

_____

APPLES of GOLD
in BASKETS
of SILVER
Proverbs 25:11

Lord, help me to never become weary doing good. I want to always remember that I am sowing seed that will produce a harvest not only for me, but for many others, too. I want to be doing well by being fair, conferring benefits, and cheering up others every day. Amen

Golden Apple Eight

The Fruit of Faithfulness

"Woe to you, teachers of the law and Pharisees, you hypocrites! You give a tenth of your spices—mint, dill and cummin. But you have neglected the more important matters of the law—justice, mercy and faithfulness. You should have practiced the latter, without neglecting the former."

(Matthew 23:23, *NIV*)

*O*ur God is ever faithful to His Word and to His people. His Word says that He cannot be anything else. Faithfulness is the attribute and attitude displayed in the one in whom faith can be placed. The Greek word for faithfulness in the above verse means trustworthy and faithful in the transactions of life and the execution of religious duties—reliable in all ways.

Do others know that they can always trust in and rely upon you? People today have become quite careless about being trustworthy and faithful. Promises are not kept, excuses are made, and appointments are neglected without any remorse. The reason given for this is often, *"Oh, I'm sorry. My plans changed. I guess I should have called. Let's set another date, okay?"*

We represent the most high God to the world. This means that we must always try to maintain very high standards in our lives. We should always keep our word, even when it would inconvenience us or cause us loss. We should always be kind and helpful. We should always be honest and truthful. We must watch carefully that we do not rationalize doing what everyone else is doing today, things that the disciples of the New Testament would never consider doing.

Lord, I am going to watch my words and deeds so I can catch any sneaky trick of my soul. I want to be known as a Christian who closely resembles the character of my Father. Amen.

Tasting The Truth

What does Jesus say (in Matthew 23:23) are the more important matters other than tithes and sacrifices?

_____

_____

_____

What is faithfulness?

_____

_____

What did faithfulness mean in the original Greek language?

_____

_____

_____

Would people describe you as being filled with the fruit of faithfulness? Explain your answer.

_____

_____

_____

_____

What Scripture in the Word tells us that we are not to do what everyone else in the world does? Write it out here.

_____

_____

APPLES of GOLD
in BASKETS
of SILVER
Proverbs 25:11

I want to be known as faithful and true. Lord, help me to know what I have done that has hurt people. Help me to remember them and to do what I can to make amends. Forgive me, and I ask that you give them grace to forgive me. Teach me how to always be faithful in everything I say and do. Check me when I say I am going to do something that I know I won't. Hold me to a higher standard than the world, Lord. Amen.

Golden Apple Nine

The Fruit of Gentleness

*"And the servant of the Lord must not strive; but be gentle unto all men,
apt to teach, patient, in meekness instructing those that oppose
themselves; if God peradventure will give them repentance
to the acknowledging of the truth."*

(2 Timothy 2:24-25, *KJV*)

Is the fruit of gentleness apparent in your life in this day of grabbing all you can get because you only "go around once"?

The original Greek describes the gentleness of Christ (always the best example), as a suitable, fair attitude of clemency. Christ's gentleness was not necessarily a quiet, shy reaching out to touch lives. It was a strong and supportive attitude of clemency meaning compassion, forgiveness, forbearance, kindness, and mercy.

In Second Timothy 2:24-26 (*NAS*), Paul says, *"The Lord's bond-servant must not be quarrelsome, but be kind to all, able to teach, patient when wronged, with gentleness correcting those who are in opposition."* It is not always easy to want to be gentle with those who oppose you when you are working towards a good goal. But in Proverbs 25:15, we read, *"Through patience a ruler can be persuaded, and a gentle tongue can break a bone."* Patience waits for a good opportunity to offer reasons and then gives people time to consider them. The gentle tongue speaks without provocation and can often sneak up on the roughest soul. Gentleness is a very versatile fruit that wears well.

Lord, your Word says that I should always be prepared to give an answer to everyone who asks me why I hope in you, and I am to answer them with gentleness and respect. I commit myself to doing this. Help me to answer everyone with the gentle fruit of the Spirit, in kindness and gentleness. Amen.

Tasting The Truth

The gentleness of Christ is described how in the original Greek language?

_____

_____

_____

Give an example of how this kind of gentleness could touch someone's life.

_____

_____

_____

How do you gently correct those who are opposing you? List some ways you can practice trying to do this.

_____

_____

_____

_____

Give an example of how a gentle tongue could "sneak up" on the roughest soul.

_____

_____

_____

Give an example of combining gentleness with firmness.

_____

_____

Show me how to be gentle and firm, gentle and kind, gentle and productive. I know that your Holy Spirit can reconcile the sweet fruit of Jesus' life with good communication skills. I want to act gentle, speak gentle, and walk softly. I want others to hardly know I've been teaching them about the love of Christ until its too late and they are overwhelmed by it. Amen.

Golden Apple Ten

The Fruit of Self-Control

*"Make every effort to add to your faith goodness; and to goodness,
knowledge; and to knowledge, self-control; and to self-control, perseverance;
and to perseverance, godliness; and to godliness, brotherly kindness;
and to brotherly kindness, love. For if you possess these qualities in
increasing measure, they will keep you from being ineffective
and unproductive in your knowledge
of our Lord Jesus Christ."*

(2 Peter 1:5-8, *NIV*).

The fruit of self-control, or temperance, is described in the original Greek as the virtue of being able to master the desires and passions of the soul and the flesh. The lack of self-control is one of the traits that is warned of as being rampant in the last days.

One of the most comforting things of the fruit of the Spirit is that they already exist within the born-again spirits of all believers—resident within the Incorruptible Seed of Christ's life that we received at the new birth. Even if you feel like the weakest Christian in the world, the one who is never able to say no to temptation, you can take heart. All you need to do is make room in your soul for this fruit to take root.

The human soul goes to great lengths to block this particular fruit from creeping into its control center. Our souls do not see the fruit of the Spirit as being helpful, rather they perceive anything of God to be restrictive, especially since self-control is our response to God's desire for our obedience.

Lord, I desire to be self-controlled and focused in all that do. I bind my will to your will and I loose all deception and denial from my soul in order to make room for self-control to grow and flourish within my soul. I do not want to be out of control at any time, unless I abandon myself to your love. Amen.

Tasting The Truth

How is the fruit of self-control described in the original Greek language?

_____

_____

_____

_____

How do you get this fruit from your spirit to your soul?

_____

_____

_____

Why do our souls resent the fruit of the Spirit?

_____

_____

_____

Second Timothy 3:2-5 tells us what people without any self-control act like. List these attributes and attitudes.

_____

_____

_____

Self-control is our response to what?

_____

_____

Self-control is a fruit that I definitely need and desire to be rooted down within my soul. I bind my will to your will, Lord, and I loose all of my soul's opposition to this transfer of your fruit from my spirit. Lack of self-control in these last days will cause much grief and pain to many. I ask that you would help many Christians grow in this fruit to help offset that grief and pain with good examples and love. Help me encourage others to make room to receive this same fruit. Amen.

Silver Basket

CHOICES & CONSEQUENCES

Golden Apple One

Making Choices Is Like Sowing Seeds

"Whatsoever a man sows, that and that only is what he will reap."

(Galatians 6:7, *Amplified*)

As believers, we are faced with choices every day. Each choice we make produces consequences—good or bad. Choices are the options your soul perceives to be available to it and the selections it makes based upon them. Consequences are the benefits and blessings or the burdens and penalties that result from your choices. With every choice you make, you sow seed that <u>will</u> produce a harvest some day—guaranteed! Unfortunately, it doesn't help to pray for crop failure.

Your past is all about the choices you have already made. Because of their consequences, you may still be dealing with weeds and thistles from past sowing. The good news is that you can learn powerful, decision-making skills for the future from those wrong choices. And, you still have an unimaginable realm of other good choices ahead of you—regardless of the bad seeds you have sown. Isn't that good news?

You cannot undo your past choices, but you do not have to continue living under the pain and fear they initially produced. You can allow the Holy Spirit to neutralize all past painful memories and the ensuing ragged emotions that grew from them. Then you can choose to archive them in your memory bank as neutral historical facts after having learned from them. They will have no more power to hurt or frighten you.

Lord Jesus, I bind my mind to your mind. I loose all of the strongholds I have built and the guard walls I have erected to try to control the consequences of my wrong choices. Help me learn from them, surrendering to your work in me as a good result of going through the school of consequences. Amen.

Tasting The Truth

What are choices?

_____

_____

_____

What are consequences?

_____

_____

_____

What has defined your life until now?

_____

_____

_____

What can you learn from wrong choices?

_____

_____

_____

What should you do so you do not have to live in fear and pain from your past wrong choices?

_____

_____

_____

_____

APPLES of GOLD
in BASKETS
of SILVER
Proverbs 25:11

Thank you for the Keys of the Kingdom. I want to make right choices from this day on, so I bind my will to your will, Father. I am in the midst of a harvest of consequences now. It is not pleasant, but I trust you to teach me from them. I loose all of the wrong attitudes I have had about these consequences and all of the wrong patterns of thinking I've recycled over and over about how get out of them. I want to learn what I need to know now so I don't have to go through them again. Amen.

Golden Apple Two

Breaking Negative Reaping Cycles

"For he who sows to his flesh will of the flesh reap corruption,
but he who sows to the Spirit will of the
Spirit reap everlasting life."

(Galatians 6:8, *NKJV*)

Sometimes others sow seeds into our lives that impact our thinking and our actions. The consequences of such sowing belong to them. However, we must break the sowing and reaping cycle we initiate and perpetuate when we verbally and mentally keep rehearsing and thereby reinforcing the anger, unforgiveness, confusion, and fear still in our souls! What happened to you in your past lives on today only in your memories. These memories (which can be electrified by emotions, fears, and skewed perceptions) provide the power your unsurrendered soul draws upon to control your life.

Counseling, support, and love can help you learn to cope with old memories, but nothing can ever "neutralize" the power they exert over you except the grace of God. Begin your healing by voluntarily destroying the strongholds and defense systems your soul has built to try to control those painful memories.

When you choose to give Him access, He will neutralize the sting of old memories by the greater power of His grace. You do this by loosing the wrong beliefs, unhealthy attitudes, unforgiveness, and strongholds your soul has put up between you and intimate knowledge of Him. He will not destroy your defense systems and He will not wipe out your old memories. How would you know what He had done for you if He did?

Father, I do not want to try to protect and hide my bad memories any longer. I bind my will to yours and I loose all of my self-defense systems to give you full access to my deepest parts. Come in to my soul and heal me. Amen.

Tasting The Truth

What have you learned from this Golden Apple?

_____

_____

Seeds of wrong choices sown into our lives by others produce consequences that do not belong to us. Explain this sentence.

_____

_____

What do we do that perpetuates the growing of negative harvests that we did not sow into our lives?

_____

_____

What seems to "supercharge" your most frightening memories?

_____

_____

Compare the results counseling often produces with the results of the grace of God when applied to old memories.

_____

_____

How do you give God access to get past your strongholds and defense systems to get to your deepest and oldest pain?

_____

_____

APPLES of GOLD
in BASKETS
of SILVER
Proverbs 25:11

Lord, I declare that this is the day that I begin stopping my thoughts when my soul wants to rerun tapes about my past, and I will bind my mind to the mind of Christ and think about Him. I will "unlearn" my soul's recycling methods and let you into its pain. I will forgive those from my past who hurt me. Amen.

Golden Apple Three

Choosing Life And Good

"I have set before you today life and good, death and evil, in that I command you today to love the LORD your God, to walk in His ways, and to keep His commandments, His statutes, and His judgments, that you may live and multiply . . . therefore choose life, that both you and your descendants may live; that you may love the LORD your God, that you may obey His voice, and that you may cling to Him, for He is your life and the length of your days."

(Deuteronomy 30:15-16, 19-20, *NKJV*)

Today, choose life and good! Choose life for yourself and your descendants, and choose to speak life to others. Thank your Lord for giving you such choices. Thank Him for clearly showing you in this Scripture how simple your choices are.

Your choices impact your life and the lives of those who love you. Choose to declare to yourself and to God that you will not choose to use any chemical substance, nicotine, alcohol, wrong behavior, bad habit, wrong relationship, fornication, or soul tie to help your soul convince itself that it is well. Only God can make everything well within your soul!

Choose to refuse to allow your soul to engage in any more wrong mind/body agreements or destructive patterns of behaviors. Choose to turn to Jesus in prayer when you begin to worry and feel stressed. Choose to worship your heavenly Father and abide in His unconditional love. Choose to read the Word and receive its empowerment and strength to keep your soul from making wrong choices in attempts to stop its pain.

Jesus, I'm choosing you over past patterns of behavior that I have always turned to. I will choose to pray, worship, and read your Word daily. I will choose life daily, and I will obey the Father's statutes and commandments, for life is in them. Amen.

Tasting The Truth

The previous Scripture says that you should obey His voice and cling to Him because:

_____

_____

_____

Who do your wrong choices impact?

_____

_____

What are some of the destructive behaviors that the soul uses to dull its pain and deny its struggles?

_____

_____

_____

What should you choose to do to stop your soul's attempts to fix its own pain?

_____

_____

_____

List any destructive behavior patterns that you recognize as attempts by your soul to lessen its pain and help its denial. Commit yourself to praying about these every day, asking God for strength, direction, and truth.

_____

_____

_____

APPLES of GOLD in BASKETS of SILVER Proverbs 25:11

Thank you, Lord, for giving me simple choices to make: just choose life or death, obedience or disobedience. Please remind me that every choice I make this day comes back to life or death, obedience of disobedience. Help me to remember that my choices always impact others, too. I call my soul's lies for what they are and I loose all agreement with them. I am choosing to do things your way from now on so that I might have life and be blessed. I want everything you have. Amen.

Golden Apple Four

Choosing Right Words

*"Watch the way you talk. Let nothing foul or dirty come out of your mouth.
Say only what helps, each word a gift."*

(Ephesians 4:29, *The Message*)

Carefully consider the words you choose to speak today. Spoken words have great power to either bless or curse. Being able to speak has never meant you were free to say anything you wanted to. So many people today feel that freedom of speech means they have a right to spew out hurtful words of perversion, violence, and hatred over the Internet, in music, in movies and television, and in magazines and books. Words have become cheap, and few understand how they can feed evil.

It is a sin for believers to speak words that tear down and discourage. Choose this day to begin to speak only words that help and promote the well being of others. Choose this day to make sure that all of your words are a gift to those who hear them—rather than a burden. In 1 Thessalonians 1:8, Paul commends the Thessalonian Christians, saying, *"The news of your faith in God is out. We don't even have to say anything anymore—you're the message!"* (*The Message*).

You are the message and the messenger that the omnipotent God of the universe and beyond has chosen to send to the world. Choose to share good words, not negative ones.

Father, please help me be aware of every word I say today. If my words will not inspire, encourage, and bless, help me to remain silent. It is better to be silent and thought wise and kind than to open my mouth and prove I'm not. Teach me how to be an encourager and a blessing to others. I loose all previous wrong patterns of thinking and generational bondage thinking that have contributed to my speaking negative or unkind words. I want to speak life to all who hear my voice. Amen.

Tasting The Truth

What did you learn from this Golden Apple?

_____

_____

How do you think a word or words can be a gift to someone?

_____

_____

_____

How do you think words can feed evil?

_____

_____

It is better to be silent and thought wise and kind than to open your mouth and prove you are not. What does this mean to you?

_____

_____

How do you think generational thought patterns learned throughout your whole life can contribute to speaking negative words?

_____

_____

What gift of words could you give to everyone you meet today?

_____

_____

APPLES of GOLD
in BASKETS
of SILVER
Proverbs 25:11

Jesus, I do want to consider my words more carefully. I forget the power within them to bless or to curse. Help me remember that I don't have the right to say anything that tears another person down. I have been given the gift of speech to build up and encourage myself and others. You gave me speech to praise you out loud, and bless you and others. Amen.

Golden Apple Five

No More Fear Of Making Choices

"I have set my heart on your laws. I hold fast to your statutes, O LORD; do not let me be put to shame. I run in the path of your commands, for you have set my heart free."

(Psalm 119:30-32, *NIV*)

The Bible does not just contains verses about eternity and getting into heaven as some think, it is also rich with advice and direction on how to choose the best paths and ways right here on earth.

When a child grows up feeling that his or her choices frequently seemed to produce negative consequences, there is little motivation to learn how to make "right" choices. Decisions avoided seem to be negative consequences deflected. Acts of procrastination can easily be rationalized as safe semi-solutions, rather than indecision.

Some people choose to live with procrastination's stress rather than that spiking of fear that a decision could be wrong. Some even choose to ignore urgent decisions that should be made, letting them progress to "natural" conclusions that often involve great fallout. This person would rather clean up the fallout than try to make right choices that would avert the damage in the first place. Doing nothing is a choice, too, and can be a very wrong one. Wisdom comes from learning to make right choices. Do not be afraid of wrong decisions while you are learning, but trust the Lord to teach you from them.

Lord, I bind my will to your will, and I loose all fear and doubt I have about making choices. I do not want to just be a "damage control expert." Show me the principles of choosing well that are seemingly hidden within your Word— principles that even clarify today's decisions that aren't found in the Bible. Help me to learn how to use these principles. Amen.

Tasting The Truth

The Bible contains what kinds of verses?

_____

_____

_____

What tends to kill any motivation for learning to make right decisions?

_____

_____

_____

What do decisions avoided become to the person who is fearful of making choices?

_____

_____

A person who chooses to ignore even urgent decisions is generally choosing to do what?

_____

_____

Refusing to make a choice is a choice. What does this mean?

_____

Can you learn wisdom from making both wrong choices and right choices?

_____

_____

APPLES of GOLD in BASKETS of SILVER Proverbs 25:11

Lord, if I've been procrastinating, help me to change. I loose all fear I have about making wrong choices. I know I need to practice making right choices, and I ask you to help me do so. I bind my mind to your mind, Jesus. I ask that you guide me in every choice I make from now on. If I am completely unsure of what to choose, then I will wait to hear your voice. I will believe that you are going to speak. Amen.

Golden Apple Six

You Always Have A Choice

"I will instruct you and teach you in the way you should go;
I will guide you with My eye."

(Psalm 32:8, *NKJV*)

The statement, "I had no choice," is simply not true—whether the consequences may be dangerous to our lives or just uncomfortable to our pride. Even if our only choice left is to die before a firing squad with our heads high and praising God or to scream in fear and curse Him, we always have a choice!

We look at many of our tough choices through a veil of anxiety and apprehension: How am I going to be personally affected by the results of this choice? God looks at our tough choices as either a miracle-producing process of acting by faith or a hard trip back around Mt. Sinai process of not acting by faith.

Anxiety is God's pager alerting us that it's time to talk to Him about a situation that is worrying us. When anxiety threatens, God invites us to come to Him in prayer, promising that He will work with us. He knows we're faced each day with temptation, frustration, and a tendency to want to make choices that seem to promise the easy way out.

Every day is another opportunity to test our decision-making skills. Every day is another opportunity to make right decisions that don't consider any easy way out. One thing I have found out about the lessons God wants to teach me is that I often forget the ones that come easy. Sometimes I have to relearn them over and over. The lessons that stretch me and push me out of my comfort zone are the ones I rarely forget.

Lord, I accept the truth that I always have a choice, I just don't always like the choices I have. Today I will try to view my choices from your perspective, and make the right ones. Amen.

Tasting The Truth

"I had no choice" is never true. Explain why.

_____

_____

_____

What do we often think when we are facing a tough choice?

_____

_____

How does God look at our tough choices?

_____

_____

_____

Anxiety should be viewed as what?

_____

_____

_____

God invites and promises what regarding choices?

_____

_____

Compare the usual outcomes of easy lessons and hard lessons.

_____

_____

APPLES of GOLD in BASKETS of SILVER Proverbs 25:11

I believe that you will instruct, teach, and guide me in all I do when I bind my will to yours, Lord. I choose to believe that I always have a choice that can be made to please you. I know how stressful I feel when I look at my toughest decisions, but I will choose to now see them as you see them—a miracle-producing process of my acting by faith. Amen.

Golden Apple Seven

Choose Life

"The thief comes not except to steal, and to destroy. I have come that they may have life, and that they may have it more abundantly. I am the good shepherd. The good shepherd gives His life for the sheep."

(John 10:10-11, *NKJV*)

Believers who depend on God are called the sheep of His pasture. Jesus came as the Good Shepherd of God's sheep to bring them to abundant life. Sheep are harmless; meek and quiet, patient, useful and profitable, tame, sociable one with another, and much used in sacrifices. As His sheep, we are to continually sacrifice our rights and our wills to Him.

Jesus came to give us life abundant, life with great advantage right now. Why do so many people think that they will find a more exciting life in the world, in the honky tonks, in the dance halls, or in the adult movie theaters? What has blinded them to the peace, the promise, and the love in the life He offers. The god of this world, Satan, has blinded them.

When any thing threatens to steal His life in us, we must hold it tight, affirm it, confirm it, and agree with God that it is ours. His life is our non-refundable gift from Jesus Christ, himself. We are the only ones who can separate us from His life until God is ready to graduate us to life in heaven with Him.

"Jesus said . . . 'I am the way, the truth, and the life. No one comes to the Father except through Me'" (John 14:6, *NKJV*). He is our back stage pass to the Father, our identification card to get through to God's truth and glorious life.

Thank you, Jesus, for giving me choices that are glorious indeed. I choose all that is in you—your way, God's truth, and abundant life with favor and advantage here on earth. Amen.

Tasting The Truth

Describe the attributes of sheep.

_____

_____

What is our main sacrifice to God today?

_____

_____

_____

Why do you think so many people reject the life in Christ and turn to the artificial life/death of the world's ways?

_____

_____

How can we separate ourselves from His life even temporarily?

_____

_____

Write Jesus a short thank you letter right here for giving you abundant life.

_____

_____

_____

Read John 10:1-18 and write down the point in this parable that most touches your heart.

_____

_____

Thank you for making it possible for me to have life abundantly, life with advantage. Please show me how to become more effective at sharing this abundant advantage with people who have been deceived by the enemy. I want to show them the truth and help them loose his deception. Amen.

Golden Apple Eight

No Punishment In God's Perfect Love

"There is no fear in love. But perfect love drives out fear, because fear has to do with punishment. The one who fears is not made perfect in love."

(1 John 4:18, *NIV*)

Have you ever had a time when you were absolutely sure that God really loved you, Jesus Christ really had made you free, and the bondage of your past was over? Then did uneasiness creep slowly in on you, discouraging and frightening you, dissolving the peace you had hoped would last?

If you really believed that God knew everything and loved you unconditionally, would you lose your God-peace over a bad doctor's report? Would you lose your God-love because your spouse said he/she didn't love you anymore? Would you lose your God-joy over a harsh word from someone else?

Most Christians repeatedly lose these God-gifts because they do not know how to refuse to agree with the negative circumstances that will come into all of our lives. We truly do have a reflex reaction that causes us to turn our magnifying glasses on the circumstances and magnify them instead of magnifying the Lord as the Word tell us to.

Often this reflex reaction is rooted in unresolved issues and guilt. When we try to bury or deny them, we set up hot buttons that the enemy loves to stomp on. Guilt is connected with fear of punishment and loss. God's perfect love has no fear of punishment in it. If His love is not compatible with guilt or punishment, something has to go. So, loose that guilt.

What is this ugly deception that is making me fearful of what you think of me? The Word says there is no fear in your love. So please help me get this straightened out in my soul. Amen.

Tasting The Truth

Perfect love drives out fear, because fear has to do with punishment. Explain this sentence.

_____

_____

Have you experienced times when you felt very high on God one day, but you felt discouraged and uneasy the next day? How did that make you feel about your knowledge of God?

_____

_____

Why do so many Christians repeatedly lose their God-gifts so quickly?

_____

_____

If the Word says He loves you and there is no room in His love for fear, yet you are full of fear—write a prayer here and ask God to show you where you are out of sync with Him. Write down what He says.

_____

_____

_____

_____

Write a short prayer here choosing to keep your magnifying glass turned on the Lord, not on your circumstances.

_____

_____

_____

APPLES of GOLD
in BASKETS
of SILVER
Proverbs 25:11

Lord, I think I have a reality glitch in my soul. I know you love me, but I struggle with fear of your disapproval. Please help me to see the truth and let your love be perfected in me. Amen.

Golden Apple Nine

Punishment, Consequences, Or Discipline?

"God disciplines us for our good, that we may share in his holiness. No discipline seems pleasant at the time, but painful. Later on, however, it produces a harvest of righteousness and peace for those who have been trained by it."

(Hebrews 12:10-11, *NIV*)

*P*unishment is generally used in the New Testament to describe eternal damnation for the unrighteous. Punishment is connected with avenging, revenge, and penalties. It also describes the self-inflicted punishment that comes from fear (1 John 4:18).

Consequences are the natural outcome of any choice that is made. The nature of the consequence relates to the nature of the choice. When you make a wrong choice, the consequence will seem to have a negative outcome. However, hard consequences can actually teach us how to make good choices better than any classroom instructor can.

Discipline (chastisement, chastening) is correction, instruction, and nurturing (original Greek). Paul said, *"If we would judge ourselves, we should not be judged. But when we are judged, we are chastened of the Lord, that we should not be condemned with the world"* (1 Corinthians 11:31-32, *KJV*). When God judges the unrighteous, He condemns them. When He judges those who believe in Christ, He corrects, instructs, and nurtures them so that they will not remain in that state of judgment. We must learn to see that His discipline is His love perfecting us.

God <u>disciplines</u> and chastens His own, He <u>punishes</u> those who have rejected His Son, and we cause our own <u>consequences</u>.

Help me to always recognize your discipline as love. Forgive me for believing it was punishment. I want to be trained in your ways to choose wisely. I love you, Lord. Amen.

Tasting The Truth

Describe the general use of the word punishment in the New Testament.

_____

_____

Describe the origin and the nature of consequences.

_____

_____

_____

Discipline is described as:

_____

_____

_____

When God judges His people, He does what?

_____

_____

What is it that perfects His love in us so that we get it right once and for all that He really loves us?

_____

_____

Compare discipline, punishment, and consequences here.

_____

_____

_____

_____

APPLES OF GOLD
in BASKETS
of SILVER
Proverbs 25:11

I will remember to always thank you for your loving discipline and for the nature of your loving judgment of your people. I would never want to be condemned with those of the world who have rejected your warnings and chastisement. Please continue to teach me to understand when I am being disciplined by you or I am walking out the consequences of my own choices. Amen.

Golden Apple Ten

If You Love Him, What Will You Choose?

"You are my friends if you do what I command. I no longer call you servants, because a servant does not know his master's business. Instead, I have called you friends, for everything that I learned from my Father I have made known to you. You did not choose me, but I chose you and appointed you to go and bear fruit—fruit that will last."

(John 15:14-16, *NIV*)

How do we show Him our love? More than verbally repeating it to Him every day, we show Him our love by obeying His commands. Some people might obey Him out of fear of retribution or because of hope of gain. His own obey Him because they love Him. He has blessed us with the intimacy of calling us His friends. What a friend we have in Jesus!

He has asked us to go and bear fruit—fruit that will last. Fruit is actually the outward and visible expression of the power working within a person. If we are to produce spiritual fruit that lasts, then we are to be effective beyond just words of witnessing and sharing our testimony. If we are just speaking words, once we cease to speak them then it will be as if those listening were looking in a mirror and then forgot what our words were when they walked away.

Jesus evidently had expectations that those who were His would speak and walk with an intimate understanding of His life and power. That life and power is to be transferred through our words so that permanent fruit will be born in others who will then surrender and submit to Him. Let us all aspire to speaking with His power and His life.

I'm willing to be willing, Lord. Help me to reprioritize those things which you have asked me to do. I want to go and speak with power and life that permanent fruit would result. Amen.

Tasting The Truth

Jesus calls us His friends because we do what He tells us to do. What does that mean to you?

_____

_____

What is the most powerful way we have of showing Him that we love Him?

_____

_____

Compare those who obey Him for wrong reasons with those who obey Him for the right reason.

_____

_____

What is the fruit Jesus is speaking of?

_____

_____

Jesus evidently had expectations that we would do what?

_____

_____

His life and power is to be transferred to our words for what?

_____

_____

What makes fruit last(clue: multiplication)?

_____

_____

APPLES of GOLD in BASKETS of SILVER Proverbs 25:11

You have chosen me and appointed me to go and bear fruit. Lasting fruit comes from the act of transferring your life to others. Thank you, Jesus, for the honor of being called to do this. I want you to know I love you, so I am choosing to set my will to obey your every wish. I want to bear lasting fruit. Amen.

10

Silver Basket

PREPARING FOR TRANSITION

Golden Apple One

The Curse Is Over, The Blessing Has Come

"He was with God in the beginning . . . In him was life, and that life was the light of men. The light shines in the darkness, but the darkness has not understood it."

(John 1:1-5, *NIV*)

*T*he Old Testament ended with the threat of a curse: *"I will send you the prophet Elijah before that great and dreadful day of the LORD comes. He will turn the hearts of the fathers to their children, and the hearts of the children to their fathers; or else I will come and strike the land with a curse"* (Malachi 4:5-6, *NIV*).

John's Gospel of the New Testament began with blessing: The One who was with God in the beginning had life in Him to give, life that would be the light of men. That light would shine in the darkness whether the darkness understood it or not.

The Law of the Old Testament was given to warn of the results of sin. The Good News of the New Testament has been given to draw people to Christ that they might have His love and life. The Good News expresses the truth of Jesus Christ's law of love being ready to come into hearts that would receive it.

Jesus Christ came not only to give us His great love, He also came to invoke blessings upon us with His full authority. He is one with the Father—He is the One who made himself man to purchase our deliverance from punishment and judgment. The everyday struggles of our human existence should dim when we focus on the fact that we were created to complete His mighty work by taking the same Good News to others.

Jesus, once again I am awed by your sacrifice to include me in your plans for salvation and redemption for mankind. I will lift my eyes up to you and follow you wherever you lead. Amen.

200

Tasting The Truth

What would cause the curse of the last verse in the Old Testament to come upon the land?

_____

_____

What was the blessing that John related in the first few verses of the Gospel of John?

_____

_____

Why was the Law of the Old Testament given and what made it necessary at that time?

_____

_____

Why was the Good News of the New Testament given?

_____

_____

_____

Jesus, who was one with the Father, sacrificed His divinity to do what?

_____

_____

Why should this cause us to stop focusing on our everyday struggles?

_____

_____

APPLES of GOLD
in BASKETS
of SILVER
Proverbs 25:11

Thank you, Father, for allowing me to be born under the New Testament covenant. Thank you for showing me the life that could be mine. Your Good News drew me to the love you would give to all who would receive your Son. I will not let my everyday existence keep me from sharing my experience with His life and the light that shines from it day and night. Amen.

Golden Apple Two

Coming Out Of The Desert Experience

"Remember how the LORD your God led you all the way in the desert these forty years, to humble you and to test you in order to know what was in your heart, whether or not you would keep his commands."

(Deuteronomy 8:2, *NIV*)

Moses spent 40 years in the desert before God launched him into his work for His Kingdom. In a believer's life today that desert experience represents the times when a Christian feels set aside and God seems mysteriously absent.

Many Christians undergoing this experience feel that nothing is happening spiritually. This is far from true, for God is working on them as well as behind the scenes arranging position and favor for their destiny purposes. He is also giving His people survival training to ensure their success in His purposes.

When God called Moses out of his desert experience, he was prepared for leading the Israelites out of Egypt through the desert because he had experience with desert survival. When God called Joseph out of his "desert experience" in prison, He positioned him with favor and power in high places in Egypt so that he would be able to lead his family through the famine.

When their desert experiences had accomplished His work in each of their hearts, these men stepped into their Kingdom positions for God. Desert experiences are preparation and pruning times, times of being readied for power. Tell the Father you want to learn everything He has for you in the desert.

Lord, I want every desert appointment of my life to work deeply in me. I want to learn what I need to know that I cannot learn in life as usual. I'm yours, Father, prepare me for my reason for living—my obedience to your plans and purposes. Amen.

Tasting The Truth

What did God tell the Israelites He was doing during their 40 years in the desert?

_____

_____

_____

What do the different "desert experiences" recorded in the Bible represent to the believer today?

_____

_____

What is God usually doing behind the scenes of these experiences?

_____

_____

_____

Once the desert experience time was over, Moses and Joseph and Jesus all moved right into their purposes. How can you relate this to your life?

_____

_____

_____

_____

What is God usually doing in the person who is in the desert experience?

_____

_____

_____

APPLES OF GOLD
in BASKETS
of SILVER
Proverbs 25:11

Thank you for the training sessions that we are allowed to experience out of the sight of the world. It is not a bad thing to be able to be pruned in private. Help me to remember that you are always right there even if I don't know what is going on. Thank you for paving my purpose with favor. Amen.

Golden Apple Three

Jesus' Desert Experience

"Jesus came from Nazareth of Galilee, and was baptized by John in the Jordan. And immediately, coming up from the water, He saw the heavens parting and the Spirit descending upon Him like a dove. Then a voice came from heaven, 'You are My beloved Son, in whom I am well pleased.' And immediately the Spirit drove Him into the wilderness. And He was there in the wilderness forty days, tempted by Satan, and was with the wild beasts; and the angels ministered to Him."

(Mark 1:9-13, *NKJV*)

The Son of God was very human when He walked the earth to teach the people. His body got tired, hungry, and needed sleep. His human soul had to think, feel, and make choices as our souls do. His soul also had the potential to complicate any human concerns He had, intensifying the approaching horror of the end of His life.

Before God prepared to cleanse Christ's human soul from all residue of His human desires and wishes, the Father first reaffirmed His pleasure in His Son. Then He had the Holy Spirit drive Jesus into the desert wilderness because He was preparing Him for ministry and His death on the cross.

Jesus was going to be pushed to the very limits of His human soul, and every bit of His soul had to be surrendered to the Father's plan. His soul's fears, doubts, and personal desires had to be fully submitted to the Father so He could endure what had to be done to become our Savior. His desert experience shows us desert survival training in an extreme manner.

Dear Jesus, how can I ever thank you. I am learning to understand the desert experience. I will surrender my soul to God so that I can complete the work that you left here for me to do. Thank you for trusting me to get it right. I will! Amen.

Tasting The Truth

How was Jesus like us in body and soul?

_____

_____

_____

How do you think His soul had the potential to complicate His response to what He faced?

_____

_____

_____

Why did God send Jesus into the desert? What was it that He wanted cleansed from Jesus' human soul?

_____

_____

_____

Once the desert experience time was over, Moses and Joseph and Jesus all moved right into their purposes. How can you relate this to your life?

_____

_____

What is in your life that you can begin to surrender now to God without having to undergo a desert experience?

_____

_____

Thank you, Lord, for being willing to take on the self-limiting characteristics of humans that were so far below you. If you had not, then we could say that you don't really understand what we have to go through. You absolutely do know. Amen.

Golden Apple Four

Sharing All Of God's Promises To Abraham

"Therefore inheriting the promise is the outcome of faith and depends entirely on faith, in order that it might be given as an act of grace (unmerited favor), to make it stable and valid and guaranteed to all his descendants; not only to the devotees and adherents of the Law but also to those who share the faith of Abraham, who is (thus) the father of us all . . . The promises were spoken to Abraham and to his seed. The Scripture does not say 'and to seeds,' meaning many people, but 'and to your seed,' meaning one person, who is Christ."

(Romans 4:16, *Amplified*; Galatians 3:16, *NIV*)

The Promise—what a wonderful phrase that is! Every good promise in the Bible is rolled up into that expression—The Promise. Life, love, forgiveness, peace, strength, joy, healing, going to heaven, and so much more is in The Promise.

Every promise made by God to Abraham was encoded into the Incorruptible Seed of Christ's life which is now in you and me. When you plant a seed, the ground must be broken up and tilled to softness for the seed to germinate. How broken and soft is the soil of your soul? If His Seed has not yet produced its divine promise within you, the problem is your soul's soil.

You don't have to produce the promise in the Incorruptible Seed, but you do have to loosen and break up the hardness of your heart that has been preventing its germination. Your prayers of surrender and loosing can dissolve any hardness in your soul.

Father, I want The Promise to grow in me and bear fruit and life for others to share. I don't want a hard and rigid heart. I loose, smash, and crush all of the walls, defenses, bad attitudes, and deception in my soul that is keeping it from being soft enough to let the Incorruptible Seed of Christ's life grow and flourish. Till me and fill me with His life. Amen.

Tasting The Truth

Inheriting the promise of Abraham depends entirely on faith to make it guaranteed to all his descentants. What do you think this means?

_____

_____

Does reading the previous Scriptures fully convince you that the promised blessings and abundance of the Old Testament are yours because you share the faith of Abraham? Why?

_____

_____

_____

What keeps the promises of God from being fulfilled in your life as a believer?

_____

_____

_____

What has Jesus provided for you to use to begin to dissolve all hardness in your heart?

_____

_____

_____

Write a short prayer here committing to wanting to loosen and break up any hardened soil areas of your heart.

_____

_____

_____

APPLES of GOLD
in BASKETS
of SILVER
Proverbs 25:11

The way of inheriting The Promise is by faith alone which guarantees that anyone can receive it: the sick, the poor, the weak, the young and the old. Thank you for providing a plan that guarantees that no one would be left out unless they wanted to be. I don't have to fulfill The Promise, I just have to make room for it to bear fruit within me. Amen.

Golden Apple Five

Chosen To Deeply Know The Father

"At that time Jesus said, 'I praise you, Father, Lord of heaven and earth, because you have hidden these things from the wise and learned, and revealed them to little children. Yes, Father, for this was your good pleasure. All things have been committed to me by my Father. No one knows the Son except the Father, and no one knows the Father except the Son and those to whom the Son chooses to reveal him."

(Matthew 11:25-27, *NIV*)

No human being will ever know the Father except those to whom Jesus chooses to reveal Him. What a blessing to be one chosen for this revelation, but does this include everyone in the body of Christ?

The Word tells us that Christ was willing to offer the revelation of the Father to all men, but not all will want a personal experience with God. The Israelites, God's chosen people, did not want to know God up close and personal. They told Moses, *"Speak to us yourself and we will listen. But do not have God speak to us or we will die"* (Exodus 20:19, *NIV*).

Does a prayer of salvation, going to church, and paying tithes automatically mean that Jesus will choose to reveal the Father to you? I don't think so. *Vines Dictionary* tells us that *"to choose"* does not always imply rejection of what is not chosen. It implies favor for what is chosen. We are dependent upon Christ for all the revelation we have of the Father—He is our mediator with God. He most likely will choose to reveal the greatest understanding of the Father to those who surrender themselves without reservation to wanting to know Him.

Jesus, I want all of the revelation you will give to me to know the Father in all His fullness. I loose all self-agendas from my soul to make room for your revelation. Thank you for doing this. Amen.

Tasting The Truth

Do you think Jesus reveals the Father to everyone in the body of Christ? Explain your answer.

_____   _____

_____

Do you have any fear of being up close and personal with God?

_____

_____

What can you do, beyond your salvation, church attendance, and giving to foster a deeper relationship with God the Father?

_____

_____

_____

What might you have to give up, what part of your comfort zone might shrink if you surrender yourself without reservation to Him?

_____

_____

_____

Are you honestly willing to give this up? Only you and the Lord know what you are writing here.

_____

_____

_____

APPLES of GOLD
in BASKETS
of SILVER
Proverbs 25:11

I want to know the Father and I know that can only happen if you choose to reveal Him to me, Jesus. I am willing to surrender whatever must go to make room within my soul to receive more of you and the Father. I desire this very much, and I will begin to do whatever you say. I know that there is nothing else I have that will fulfill me. Thank you. Amen.

Golden Apple Six

Do What You Know To Do

"Not everyone who says to me, 'Lord, Lord,' will enter the kingdom of heaven, but only he who does the will of my Father who is in heaven."

(Matthew 7:21, *NIV*)

God's will has several basic elements you should be firmly aware of: love Him with all your heart, worship Jesus Christ, love one another (even enemies), obedience and surrender, honesty in all dealings, selflessness, and a desire to be a witness for Christ. This list may not be complete, but it gives you the basics to obey while you listen for further instruction. But what is God's will for you if your car quits on the way to a job interview? Since you won't find "car breaks down on way to job interview" in your *Strong's Concordance*, what Bible passage will tell you what God's will is for this?

If God does not speak, no ride come, and no phone is in sight, simply go back to what you do know is God's will. Begin to worship the Father in prayer, repeat your love for Jesus, and think of those you can show love to when you get back on schedule. Look around to see someone you can pray for.

In other words, begin to do what you do know is God's will. Do what seems wise and appropriate at the moment. Then, if you do not get any immediate direction, do something you know is God's will while you wait for further instructions. Doing what you know to do as His will often brings you further revelation understanding, too.

I want your will, Father, whether anyone else knows I want it or not. I will start with the list of the basics above. As I do this, I will stay attentive and listen to hear if you are giving further instruction. It is so exciting to belong to you! Amen.

Tasting The Truth

Write a short prayer here committing to practicing what you have learned from this Golden Apple.

_____

_____

_____

Name the basic elements of God's will as listed above. What would you add to this list?

_____

_____

_____

What can you do to foster a deeper relationship with God the Father?

_____

_____

What should you do when a situation arises that you do not know a Scripture for?

_____

_____

Doing what you know to do regarding God's will often brings an additional blessing. What is it?

_____

What do you feel you need to work on most in His will?

_____

Lord, if I read your Word and spend quality time with you and I still do not now what your will is in a situation, I believe now that I can do what I know to do and wait for you to tell me what to do next. That takes so much pressure off me as I'm learning how to do what is right and good. Thank you! Amen.

Golden Apple Seven

Preparing Your Mind For Spiritual Action

"Therefore, prepare your minds for action; be self-controlled;
set your hope fully on the grace to be given
you when Jesus Christ is revealed."

(1 Peter 1:13, *NIV*)

Your mind is that part of you that formulates thoughts and ideas, and it is also that part of you that sometimes seems to imitate a cat chasing its tail. It is very frustrating when your mind goes round and round in a circle, never arriving at any conclusions, never getting anywhere.

You cannot be prepared for action and ready to take advantage of opportunities God sets up for you when you cannot control your mind. The Word of God says that you are to let the mind of Christ be in your mind. I'm fairly sure that Jesus won't fight your soul's merry-go-round for the right to be one with your thoughts. This is just one of the things that you can only fully experience spiritually by cooperating with God's guidance on how to receive from Him.

Jesus will not take over your mind, except perhaps in the most extreme of cases, and the Holy Spirit does not aggressively take control of your emotions to heal them. You have to open up and surrender yourself to these divine works. As you learn how to submit your mind to Jesus, submit your will to God, and submit your emotions to the Holy Spirit, then you will begin to experience divine empowerment and blessing.

Okay, Jesus, I'm ready. I will first stabilize myself by binding my will to God's will. I now bind my mind to your mind, Jesus, and I bind my emotions to the Holy Spirit. I loose all fear and doubt of being submitted and surrendered to you. I loose all wrong patterns of thinking about trusting you with every detail of my life. I will make a way for you to come in. Amen.

Tasting The Truth

Preparing your mind for action means that you should get rid of all foolish thinking, fantasizing, and wrong patterns of thinking. How else can you prepare your mind for action?

_____

_____

To control your own mind, you need to be careful about what you feed it. What do you think this means?

_____

_____

Look up the Scripture that speaks of fixing your mind on things above and write it here. What does this Scripture mean to you?

_____

_____

First Peter 1:13 also says to be self-controlled. Are there things in your life that you are not in control of? List them here and commit to seeking the help of the Lord to subdue them.

_____

_____

Write a short thank you note to God for caring enough to work with you on overcoming those things.

_____

_____

_____

I want to be able to control my mind. I do not want it going round and round. I want to be prepared for whatever action you wish for me to take, Father. I bind my mind to the mind of Christ and I loose all of the wrong thoughts that my mind keeps running. I want to hear His thoughts. Amen.

213

Golden Apple Eight

Decreasing To Increase

"He must increase, but I must decrease."

(John 3:30, *KJV*)

The key to moving into everything God has for us—healing, revelation knowledge, the ability to work miracles, all that the Word promises to each believer—keeps coming back to one thing. This is the same thing that good preachers have been saying ever since John the Baptist said it: I must decrease so Jesus can increase within me.

The "I" here is the unsurrendered soul. The basic laws of physics tell us that two things cannot occupy the same space, i.e. the same throne, at the same time. Your unsurrendered soul's territorial rights to any part of your life must decrease, ultimately disappearing, before He can increase in you.

When you are in full-scale struggle against God's dealing with your unsurrendered soul, renewal's birthing process will be painful. Forcing your soul to decrease by surrendering its "stuff" allows more room for the life of Christ to increase within you. His increase helps you to align with God's will for your life so that those great dreams you have been afraid to even speak about can begin to come into reality. Those are God-dreams He created you to walk out.

This is way beyond the understanding of the unrenewed mind and the unsurrendered will. So don't try to think it through or make it happen, just know that your part is to decrease and obey. He will do everything—everything—else that needs to be done so that your dreams and His become reality.

I'm going to decrease. I'm going on a soul diet. No more high-calorie soul junk food. Lord, I want to lose all of my soul fat and get lean and trim—my spiritual fighting weight! Amen.

Tasting The Truth

What is a major key to moving into everything God has for you?

_____

_____

What is the "I" in this verse?

_____

_____

What must happen in your soul before Jesus Christ can increase within you?

_____

_____

What causes renewal's birthing process to be so painful sometimes?

_____

_____

What are those dreams you have that you are not even free to share with others? Write them here and ask God to confirm them to you. Write down what He says.

_____

_____

_____

Write a short prayer here asking God to reveal what you need to let go so that you can have all of His provision and power working in you as you fulfill His will.

_____

_____

I want to decrease everything of my own soul and make the room necessary to receive revelation knowledge and to be able to work miracles. I want to convince others that you are the God they've been looking for. I want to tell them I can introduce them to you. I want to be able to do whatever Jesus left for me to do. Amen.

Golden Apple Nine

His Incorruptible Seed Within You

"My counsel for you is simple and straightforward: Just go ahead with what you've been given. You received Christ Jesus, the Master; now live him. You're deeply rooted in him. You're well constructed upon him. You know your way around the faith. Now do what you've been taught. School's out; quit studying the subject and start living it! And let your living spill over into thanksgiving."

(Colossians 1:6-7, *The Message*)

The Incorruptible Seed, the life of Jesus, is in every believer: *"Having been born again, not of corruptible seed but incorruptible, through the word of God which lives and abides forever"* (1 Peter 1:23, *NKJV*). This seed is waiting within you, waiting to explode in growth.

You must go beyond just being a student of the Word and start living out His life through your life. His life in you is filled with all the answers, instructions, and Kingdom access you need to be a world changer. An apple seed needs no teaching or training to fulfill its destiny to produce apples. An apple seed has everything it needs within its own cellular structure to produce its promise: sweet fruit. No one has ever seen an apple seed feeling pressured about its promise. That seed is preset to bear fruit. You are spiritually preset to bear fruit too!

Pressure is what we feel when we are supposed to get something done and we don't know how. Jesus never showed any pressure in His ministry because He knew His Father would provide whatever He needed. Your Father promises that He'll see that everything you need is right there when you need it, too. You are a promise waiting to be fulfilled.

Father, I've already been given all I need to become your fulfilled promise in me, haven't I? What a wonderful concept, I'm already preset to succeed. Show me where to start. Amen.

Tasting The Truth

Go ahead with what you have been given. You received Jesus, now live Him. What you do you think this means?

_____

_____

Many Christians wrap themselves up in their church life and their prayer lives. This is good, but are you a Christian who is actively living out His life through your life? Explain.

_____

_____

_____

If God can program an apple seed to become a large tree capable of blossoming and then growing apples, shouldn't He be able to program the Incorruptible Seed within you to succeed? Why do you think you aren't walking in its fullness yet?

_____

_____

_____

What is pressure?

_____

_____

Do you believe that you have everything you already need within you? Tell God why you can or why you can't.

_____

_____

APPLES of GOLD
in BASKETS
of SILVER
Proverbs 25:11

Your Word is right, it is time that I graduated from "school" and went out into the world and began producing sweet fruit for you. I will never stop needing to read your Word and spend time with you, but I want to start living what I've been studying. I will always be thankful. Amen.

Golden Apple Ten

Who Were You Supposed To Be Today?

*"Do not conform any longer to the pattern of this world, but be transformed
by the renewing of your mind. Then you will be able to test
and approve what God's will is—his
good, pleasing and perfect will."*

(Romans 12:2, *NIV*)

I read a story about a Christian who had a dream. In the dream, an angel came and took the Christian to a gathering where a familiar-looking person was encouraging many, offering wonderful words of godly counsel, love, hope, and comfort. It was clear that this person was both respected and loved.

Everyone in the room was blessed by the life of Christ that seemed to continuously emanate from this Christian. The dreamer asked the angel, "Why does that person look so familiar?" The angel replied, "That is who God had always planned that you would be today." Just a story, I know, but it caused me to think. Who would I be today if I had surrendered my life to Jesus right after I was born again? If I had been in alignment with Him from that day on, who would I be today?

Is it too late for you to become the woman or the man you were supposed to be today? Yesterday's opportunities are gone, but our God is never at a loss for how to maximize what you are willing to make available to Him right now. His maximization of your cooperation with today's and tomorrow's unlimited opportunities could still overturn the course of the world. How can you not want to go for everything He could still do with your life from this day forth.

What a sobering thought, Lord. Who might I have been today if I had worked with you instead of having to always be worked on by you. I want to be your partner from now on, and I want to make a difference in the world. Amen.

218

Tasting The Truth

The world might say that you have wasted much of your life since you met Christ. Do you believe that God can redeem that time and still use you in mighty ways? Explain your answer.

_____

_____

_____

If you could choose who you were supposed to be and what you were supposed to be doing today for God, who and what would that be?

_____

_____

_____

Write a prayer of repentance here, asking God to forgive you for wasting so much time. Make a commitment to God that you will be available for what He wants from this day forward.

_____

_____

_____

Can you dare to believe that He still can bring your old dreams on line and cause them to come to pass? Explain your answer, yes or no.

_____

_____

_____

_____

APPLES of GOLD in BASKETS of SILVER
Proverbs 25:11

Lord, I know you can do anything, but I guess my struggle is would you want to. If you will give me another chance, I will do my best not to waste it. I am sorry for the time I have already lost, but I want another chance to touch as many as possible and convince them you are the God of second chances. Amen.

The Keys of the Kingdom Trilogy
by Liberty Savard

- *Shattering Your Strongholds*
- *Breaking the Power*
- *Producing the Promise*

- *Derribe sus Murallas*
  (Shattering Your Strongholds - Spanish)

Also Available

- *Shattering Your Strongholds Workbook*
- *Breaking the Power Workbook*

Other Books By Liberty Savard

- *Keys to Understanding Freedom Here and Now*
- *Keys to Understanding Relationships*
- *Keys to Understanding Soul Ties, Soul Power and Soulish Prayers*
- *Keys to Understanding Spiritual Understanding and Warfare*

- *Fear Not America*

- *Unsurrendered Soul*

List of Future
Apples of Gold In Baskets Of Silver

Apples of Gold in Baskets of Silver II - A Season of Overcoming the Past

Ten Baskets of One Hundred Golden Apple Teachings/Tasting
The Truth Questions

Basket One - Who Is God Today?
Basket Two - Who Are You Today?
Basket Three - The Power Of The Soul
Basket Four - The Power Of Words
Basket Five - Strongholds And Bondage Thinking
Basket Six - Flushing Out Old Mindsets
Basket Seven - Unmet Needs, Unhealed Hurts, And Unresolved Issues
Basket Eight - Mercy And Grace - Receiving And Giving
Basket Nine - Forgiveness - Get Out Of Jail Free Key
Basket Ten - Preparing For Transition

Apples of Gold in Baskets of Silver III - A Season of Embracing Your Destiny

Ten Baskets of One Hundred Golden Apple Teachings/Tasting
The Truth Questions

Basket One - Good Words, Good Paths, And The Good Life
Basket Two - Hope, Belief, And Faith
Basket Three - Discipline And Accountability
Basket Four - Being A Role Model
Basket Five - Serving Others
Basket Six - Truth
Basket Seven - Wisdom
Basket Eight - The Power Of Surrender And Obedience
Basket Nine - Your Destiny - His Paths
Basket Ten - Preparing For Transition

Ten Baskets of One Hundred Golden Apple Teachings/Tasting
The Truth Questions

For further information on speaking engagements, seminars, current U.S. itinerary, teaching tapes, workbooks, television programs, and free teaching newsletters published quarterly,

please contact:

Liberty Savard Ministries, Inc.
(a non-profit organization)
P.O. Box 41260
Sacramento, CA 95841-0260

Office phone   916-721-7770
Facsimile   916-721-8889

E-mail: liberty@libertysavard.com
web site: libertysavard.com